COLOURFUL CHILDREN'S LITURGIES

*To Kate and Anna
and all the children
who have helped us in the making of this book*

Anne Marie Lee & Elaine Wisdom RCE

Colourful Children's Liturgies

the columba press

First published in 1994 by
the columba press
93 The Rise, Mount Merrion, Blackrock, Co Dublin

Cover by Bill Bolger
Illustrations by Elaine Wisdom RCE
Origination by The Columba Press
Printed in Ireland by
Genprint Ltd., Dublin

ISBN 1 86507 110 3

Acknowledgements
The authors wish to acknowledge and thank the following for their sup-
port and encouragement: St Laurence's Parish, Kilmacud, Co Dublin.
Our Lady of Good Counsel Parish, Johnstown, Co Dublin. Our Lady's
School and community, Clermont, Rathnew, Co Wicklow. The RCE
community, Greenacres, Kilmacud, Co Dublin. Breid Ryan, Librarian,
Deansgrange, and a very patient husband, David Lee.

Contents

Jesus called the children to him and said,
'Let the little children come to me, and do not stop them;
for it is to such as these that the kingdom of God belongs.'
Luke 18:16

Introduction

Christian liturgy is created when a group of believers gather to share and celebrate their faith. Anything that can help these gatherings to come alive in understanding the scripture and in deepening an appreciation of the Christian mystery is to be welcomed and encouraged. It is in this belief that we offer this book as a resource for anyone involved in helping to create children's liturgy. We have concentrated on visual imaging because it seems to us that much has already been written on the tradition and use of music in liturgy.

Very few people could read in the early days of the church, and because of this, the pre-Reformation church and those of the Eastern rite, developed a great historical tradition of imaging the important Christian events through the decoration of their churches. They also used the symbolism and drama of their rites and celebrations as a means of expounding the scriptures and teaching the Christian faith.

Examples of visual imaging as an aid to worship are seen in the use of statues and of paintings, particularly in the traditional sequence known as 'The Stations of the Cross' which portrays Christ carrying his cross and the people he met along the way. The use of icons in the Eastern church is also becoming increasingly known and accepted in our Western tradition. Right up to our own times, certain churches have commissioned artists to paint or sculpt their interpretation of key Christian events to help the rest of us connect more concretely with them and their meaning for our own lives.

The area of visual imaging is rich with possibility and potential. In the field of education there is a growing awareness, acknowledgement and development in the use of drama and visual stimulation to facilitate the child's learning process.

Children love to see things unfold before their eyes. Their attention is held by colour and movement. Most exciting of all is when they can take part in the activity themselves. If you have not yet started a children's liturgy in your church, you may feel hesitant about doing so. There is no need to feel this way. Gather around you others who are interested, always include children, and involve your priest or pastor. Start with simple ideas, and as you grow in confidence you will become more adventurous. Always listen carefully to the children. They are the best creators of their liturgy.

Children have wonderful imaginations and the simplest props will take them into the story. Some of you will be lucky enough to have artistic talent among your group, but don't be put off if you haven't. If you cannot draw or paint free-hand, you can trace, enlarge, cut out, colour in or make collages from old magazines, or odds and ends of material. It is amazing what inventiveness is to be found in the most inexperienced groups where children and enthusiasm are among the motivators.

There is a great sense of joy and satisfaction in working with children in this way, especially when they are able to tell you afterwards what the celebration was all about. In that case you have done a good job! Take notes and keep the ideas for next year.

This book includes only the ideas born out of our experience. We hope what you find in it will stimulate you into coming up with your own ideas for presenting the rich themes of scripture and belief in whatever way suits the needs of your particular church group best. We have left space at the end of each chapter for you to make your own notes.

May God bless you in the work of bringing his Word to children, and we hope you will know great satisfaction and deep joy as a result of your efforts.

CHAPTER 1

Approaches to Presenting the Word

1. Story telling

A good story well told is a pleasure to listen to, for both adults and children. The gospel stories are rich in content and there is scope for scene setting and modernising. The story will be more credible if told by an adult.

The story teller should know the story well and hold eye contact with the children while telling it. Inviting the children to comment or answer questions throughout the story helps to hold their attention. Encourage the children to interact with the biblical characters. You, the story teller, might dress up for the part. However, if you do, be ready for some 'smart' children to point out that spectacles and wrist watches weren't invented yet!

People, including children, are always interested in the mundane events of other people's daily lives – what they wore, the food they ate, their work or games, their arguments and their laughter. Bible stories can be fleshed out with such detail. For example, take the story of Jonah trying to escape from God.

Jonah 1:1-17
In this story God tells Jonah to go to the city of Nineveh and speak out against it. Jonah doesn't want to go so he goes off in the other direction and his journey includes a ride on a ship to Spain. There is a great and dangerous storm and the sailors are very frightened and pray to their gods for help. They throw off some of the cargo into the sea to lessen the danger. They wake Jonah up and ask him who he is and who his god is. They draw lots to see who might have angered the gods and started this storm. Jonah draws the short straw and he admits that he is the cause of the storm because he is running away from God. He advises the sailors to throw him into the sea and the storm will abate. Reluctantly they do this, and the storm ceases. The sailors are then in fear and awe of Jonah's God and they vow to offer sacrifices to him and to serve him.

This is a very rich story. The story teller could dress as the ship's captain and tell a little about life as a sailor in those days. Describe the ship and the food and clothing of the sailors. What did they use for light at night and how did they cook? Tell the children a little bit about the gods the sailors worshipped, and how they were quite superstitious. A map of the time could be reproduced on acetate and, with the use of the overhead projector, you could show the children the distance between Joppa and Spain. As the story is told, it could be illustrated with some drawings, or use mime and props, such as a large cardboard box converted to a ship etc.

Or take the story of God calling Samuel:

1 Samuel 3: 1-21

This is the story about God calling Samuel when Samuel was a young boy living with his teacher Eli who was, at this time, almost blind. They had both gone to bed, Eli to his room, while Samuel slept in the sanctuary of the temple. God called Samuel who got up and went to Eli thinking it was he who had called. This happened three times and on the third time Eli realised God was calling Samuel and he told the boy how to respond when it happened again.

This is a lovely story which has great appeal to children. Tell them a little about how it was that young boys were handed over by their parents to the Temple to be trained to serve God. This practice has lasted in different religions even up to the present day. Two children could mime the event as the story is told. What subjects did these children learn, could they read and write or were they dependant on the oral tradition? Samuel's mother Hannah had given him to the priest, Eli, because she had longed for a son and had promised God that if she did have a son she would give him up to serve God in the Temple, and this is what did happen.

Another suitable story is the sowing of the darnel among the wheat.

Matthew 13:24-43

While talking to a crowd by the lake one day, Jesus said that the kingdom of heaven might be compared to a man who sowed good seed in his field. At night his enemies came along and sowed darnel among the good seed. Jesus goes on to tell of how the owner dealt with the situation. Afterwards, when Jesus and his group had moved away from the crowd, the disciples approached him and asked him to explain the parable. Jesus explained, the sower of the good seed is the Son of Man. The field is the world, and so on.

This parable is best told as a story as there isn't enough action in it for mime or drama. The story can be fleshed out in the telling – how worried the owner was when told about the darnel, he might lose his crop, what is darnel? etc. The story teller could dress as Jesus and be surrounded by children dressed as disciples and the crowd. When the story is finished, Jesus and his disciples could get up and move to one side for the explanation.

2. Mime

Some history

In the middle ages, a religious rite or ceremony could be called a *mystery*, hence the name Mystery Play for the dramatisation of a religious theme. Mime was the forerunner of drama and both were used extensively in the middle ages by the church to bring the faith to the people. Mystery plays were written in Latin by priests who also acted in them, along with members of trade guilds or unions. The guilds and union members took on the parts relevant to their line of work, e.g. the goldsmith guild members would play the three wise kings, the carpenters' guild members might play the part of Joseph and so on. This tradition, begun in the middle ages, is still carried on in parts of England to this day, e.g. the mystery play held at York. In the German village of Oberammergau a Passion Play has been performed by the villagers every ten years since 1634. Passion plays are also performed in the United States of America.

Advantages of Mime

By mime we mean the acting out of a scene without dialogue on the part of the actors. The mime may tell its own story or a narrator might read a story while the actors perform it. Mime enhances the message and helps the audience to remember it more clearly. Mime has advantages over drama in a church or hall where the acoustics or sound system is not effective. It gives opportunity for a wider group of children to participate and children, too young to read or memorise lines, can take part.

Examples

The following mime was performed at a children's liturgy in Dublin, Ireland:

The Theme: 'Workers in the Vineyard' Mt 20: 1-16

Props: A bale of hay in front of the altar with five garden rakes leaning against it. On the back wall above the altar was a banner saying 'Jesus Is Challenging Our Values'. To the right of the altar was a tall stand with a large orange circle on top representing sunrise to sunset.

Characters: The vineyard owner, his manager and about twelve idle labourers, all dressed in the costume of the day. The labourers were sitting around playing jackstones or standing chatting. The celebrant of the Mass read the gospel story slowly and the actors played out the scene as he spoke. The owner came to the idle workers throughout the day and bargained with them over wages for work. Those he employed took up rakes and began to work. The manager wrote the deals down in his scroll until, at the end of the day, the owner paid out the agreed wages. When the workers compared their wages they began to argue with the owner and to complain among themselves.

The whole performance was very well played and well received by the congregation. Now, you may ask, 'What were they doing with a bale of hay and garden rakes?' Well, in our country we have no vineyards, so they were setting a scene of country life and outdoor work that their congregation would be familiar with. It worked!

In Devon, England, a Nativity Play was performed at Christmas by the children of the village school in the local Anglican Church. There were soldiers, shepherds, angels, wise men, inn keepers, Mary, Joseph and the child. The mime was performed while the school sang appropriate carols illustrating the sequence of events. While the small soldiers, shepherds, etc., marched around the church searching for the baby Jesus, one child climbed the steps of the pulpit and held up a star for the wise men to see.

Every child in the school had a part to play in the performance and parents and teachers were occupied for hours ahead, rehearsing them and preparing costumes and props.

Tips

When performing a mime or drama, you can add extra characters so long as they don't alter the meaning of the piece of scripture, e.g. in the story of the wise and foolish virgins you can add a shopkeeper, his assistant and a few customers in the shop where the oil is sold. In the story of the ten lepers, you could add some officials who banish them from public areas, some onlookers and maybe a physician who examines them and declares them to be lepers. By adding extra characters you are allowing more children to take part. Also the addition of a little appropriate humour will be much appreciated.

3. Drama

A drama tells a story by means of action and speech. Simple drama has been performed since ancient times, notably in Greek culture, where it is thought to have derived from religious ceremonies.

Drama is useful in children's liturgies when the children are old enough to read, learn lines and remember them for the performance.

The public address system must be adequate and the children taught how to use it to the best advantage. Mime is the best medium where the public address system is inadequate.

The drama should be short, simple, to the point and relevant to the theme of the day. The children can be dressed up for their parts or not, depending on the story line. For example, in a drama depicting bullying in the school playground, the children would not need to dress up. For a parable from the New Testament, the children could wear costumes of the time.

While it is essential in drama and mime to have a practice time before each celebration, in order to enhance the sacredness and dignity of the occasion by having the participants well versed in their parts, it is not necessary to attain perfection. Small mistakes and bouts of nervousness are well tolerated by the congregation at a family or children's service, without loss of the essential communication.

We suggest you write your own simple scripts. Children are full of ideas and will probably write their own scripts with encouragement from you. Bring together a small group of children to work with at a time. Allow the children to use their own language, for example a group of our children wrote a Nativity Play and some of the script went as follows:

Mary and Joseph going to Bethlehem. Mary rides on a donkey. The donkey consists of two children, the one in front wearing a cardboard donkey's head, and a brown blanket is thrown over the backs of both children. Mary leans against the donkey as though riding it but she is actually walking.

'Joseph: Move along donkey, you're so slow.
Donkey: I've a terrible pain in my back. Mary is so heavy.
Joseph: Aw, come on, we're nearly there.
Donkey: No I'm not budging.
Mary: Joseph, maybe we should have a little rest? We're all quite tired..'
and so on...

Because the donkey wasn't expected to speak, this section was quite light hearted. Yet, it gave a sense of the length and hardship of the journey. It is no harm to allow a gentle sense of humour to prevail.

In the script, when Mary went to visit Elizabeth, the same group of children had Elizabeth dress with a pillow under the front of her robe to simulate pregnancy. When Elizabeth rushed out to greet Mary she stopped suddenly, held her abdomen and said, 'Oops, a kick', and then went on with the greeting. 'For as soon as I heard your greeting, the baby within me jumped with gladness' (Luke 1: 44).

If the children are writing their own scripts for drama, there will be no problem with culture or dialect as they will write as they speak. Both they and their audience will feel comfortable with the end product.

Notes on story telling/mime/drama:

CHAPTER 2

Making the Costumes

Introduction

Most playschools and many homes, where there are children, have a dressing-up box. Children will spend hours in the world of their imagination, dressing themselves up as characters from history, science fiction, television and story books. Dressing up as characters from the bible is fun, the materials are easy to come by, and the costumes are simple to make. It allows children to participate, particularly where there is a crowd scene.

In biblical times, there were wealthy people and poor people, carpenters, merchants, soldiers, priests, mothers, princesses, emperors, kings, queens, shepherds, rabbis, slaves, fishermen, farmers, children, angels and prophets.

Types of clothing

The fabric from which the people made their clothes was home-spun and, depending on their wealth, could be made from wool, cotton, linen or silk. The material was dyed with natural dyes made from plants and animals. The fixative used with some dies is called a mordant and this came from certain shellfish. So many shellfish had to be crushed for the smallest amount of purple dye that only the wealthy could afford it. Purple, therefore, was the colour worn by emperors, kings and priests. ('There was a rich man who used to dress in purple and fine linen and feast magnificently every day.' [Lk 16:19]) Purple is also the colour of vestment worn by the priest at a Mass during Lent in the Roman Catholic Church.

Colour, then, played an important part in their times, as it still does in the liturgical year of our times, and in our lives generally.

Animal skins were used for clothing and for carrying water and wine. Skins were also tanned to make leather for sandals, belts, bags and armour. Parchment, on which the scribes wrote, could also be made from animal skins. You can make paper look like parchment by holding the edge a couple of inches above a flame and browning it. Only adults should try this!

In Jesus' day, just as today, you could often tell the race, religion or profession of a person by the way they were dressed.

1. Head-Gear

Materials: Rectangular or square pieces of lightweight material in plain
        colours or striped.
        Safety pins
        Silver and coloured foil
        Card (sides of cereal packets etc)
        Staples
        Adhesive tape
        Plastic pudding bowl
        Silver tinsel
        Scissors
        Measuring tape
        Pencil/markers/crayons/paints
        Glue

These materials can be used in a variety of ways for a variety of head-gear, depending on the type of person in question. For example, silver and coloured foil can be scrunched up and stapled on to circlets of card to give the impression of precious jewels. The coloured foil from sweet wrappings is very useful here.

Card from cereal packets can be cut up and used to make head-pieces, helmets, halos and so on.

Other simpler head-wear can be made from towels, scarves, or rectangular pieces of material, tied on with lengths of cord or strips of material

The illustrations on the following pages show a range of simply-made headgear for a variety of different characters.

Circlet headpiece

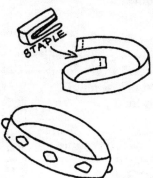

1. Cut out cardboard strip about 2"- 4" in width and staple ends securely.

2. Cover with foil.

3. Leave plain, or decorate with sweet paper jewels

Circlet for an Empress

1. Measure child's head.

2. Cut out and slot together at A.

Angel's Halo

1. A dinner-plate-sized circle of cardboard.

2. Cut inner hole, approximately the size of a small plate.

3. Cover with foil.

Soldiers' Helmets

Back & Neckguard

1. Two narrow sides
of a cereal box.
2. Cut front band with
nose-guard from one length
3. Cover with foil.

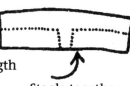

Staple together

Tip
Remember to
measure round
the child's head.

Staple → ← Staple

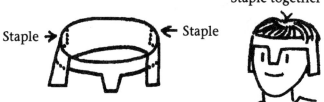

An advantage of this helmet is that it can be reversed to make
a crown   or a head dress

Crown

1. Length
of card-
board of
desired
depth.

2. Cut out
as shown.

STAPLE ENDS

3. Paint/cover with foil
and decorate with sweet
paper jewels.

2. Costumes

Materials: Old plain or striped cotton or lightweight skirts
>   Towels, large and small
>   Old sheets
>   Old curtain material, netting and lining
>   Dressing gowns
>   Men's shirts
>   Tee shirts
>   Safety pins
>   Costume jewellery – bangles, coloured beads etc
>   Old belts
>   Neck and head scarves
>   Strips of material for belts and head-bands

These materials will provide a range of types of dress which you may require, as illustrated on the following pages. Use your own creativity in adapting these to your particular needs, but here are a few general ideas to start you off:

An adult's knee-length skirt will be ankle-length on the child. If the waist-band of the skirt is worn high under the child's arms, it should be safety-pinned on to the tee shirt underneath. If worn at waist level, it can be held on with a waist-band and tied at the back.

A small towel makes a head-dress or a shawl. The large towel may be worn around the waist, as you would after a shower, with a tee shirt for a top.

Curtain material may be cut into required squares or rectangles to make shawls, cloaks or loose wrap-around garments.

Men's shirts, with sleeves and collars removed, make excellent tunics. Wrap a cloth band or belt around the waist.

Tee shirts are useful as bases onto which shawls and skirts can be safety-pinned.

Dressing gowns serve as the loose coat-like garment of the time, or they can be worn as cloaks.

Short Tunic

You can adjust the length of the tunic
by using different lengths of material.

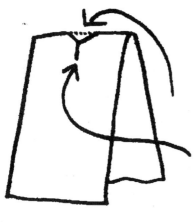

1. Long rectangle of plain or striped cloth, folded lengthways in the middle.

2. Mark middle of centre fold and cut 'V' for the child's head.

It can be enlarged by cutting a slit down the front.

3. Slip over child's head and tie at the waist. It may need to be stitched a little to prevent too much of a gap at the sides.

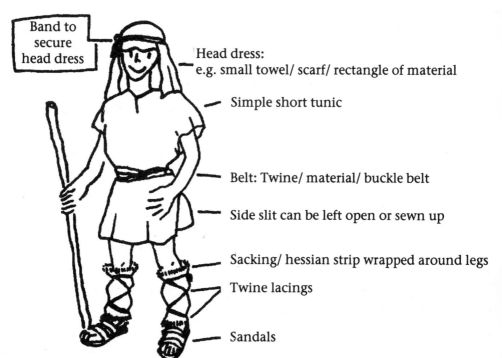

Band to secure head dress

Head dress:
e.g. small towel/ scarf/ rectangle of material

Simple short tunic

Belt: Twine/ material/ buckle belt

Side slit can be left open or sewn up

Sacking/ hessian strip wrapped around legs

Twine lacings

Sandals

Optional features   Wider scoop or 'V' neck.
Edges hemmed may be necessary on a wealthier character, otherwise they are better left rough-edged.

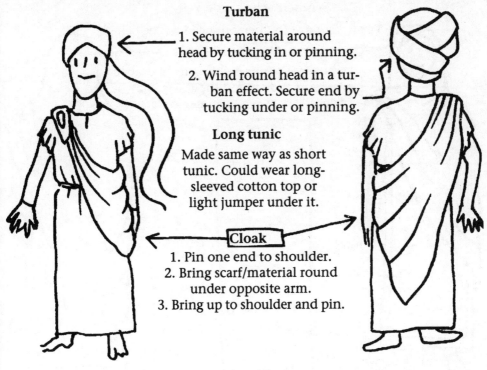

Turban

1. Secure material around head by tucking in or pinning.

2. Wind round head in a turban effect. Secure end by tucking under or pinning.

Long tunic

Made same way as short tunic. Could wear long-sleeved cotton top or light jumper under it.

Cloak

1. Pin one end to shoulder.
2. Bring scarf/material round under opposite arm.
3. Bring up to shoulder and pin.

Long tunic with sleeves

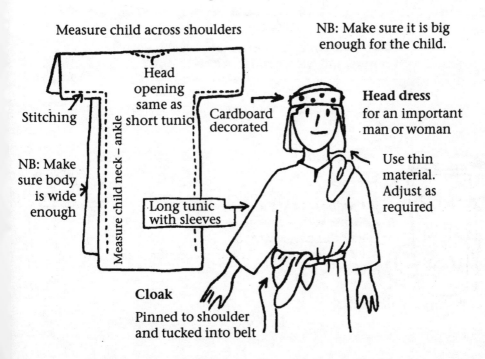

Measure child across shoulders

NB: Make sure it is big enough for the child.

Head opening same as short tunic

Stitching

Cardboard decorated

Measure child neck – ankle

NB: Make sure body is wide enough

Long tunic with sleeves

Head dress

for an important man or woman

Use thin material. Adjust as required

Cloak

Pinned to shoulder and tucked into belt

Women's tunic and veil

Tunic: Same as for men but need not be belted

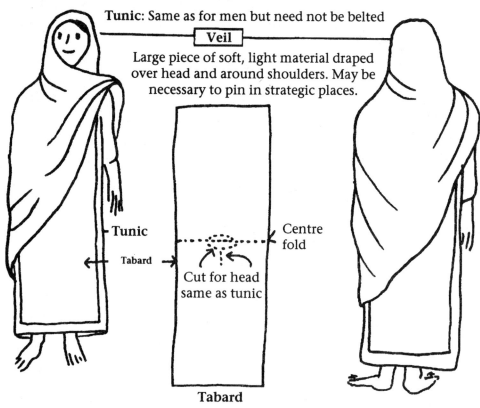

Veil

Large piece of soft, light material draped over head and around shoulders. May be necessary to pin in strategic places.

Tunic

Tabard

Centre fold

Cut for head same as tunic

Tabard

Narrow length of coloured material, put over head and left hanging back and front.

Soldiers

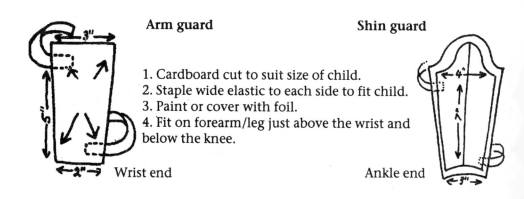

Arm guard

Shin guard

1. Cardboard cut to suit size of child.
2. Staple wide elastic to each side to fit child.
3. Paint or cover with foil.
4. Fit on forearm/leg just above the wrist and below the knee.

Wrist end

Ankle end

Soldiers

Helmet

Plastic pudding bowl with cardboard neck-guard and nose-guard taped on. Cover entire helmet with foil.

Short cloak

Attached at each shoulder, or at one and swept across throat

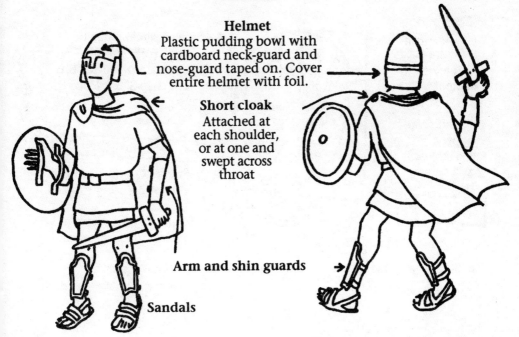

Arm and shin guards

Sandals

Costume: Large tee-shirt belted at waist, worn over material wrapped at waist and secured.

Shield

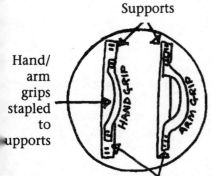

Supports

Hand/ arm grips stapled to supports

1. Washing-up bowl-sized circle of cardboard.
2. Staple on prepared cardboard arm and hand grips.
3. Cover with foil or paint.
NB: Early Roman shields were quite small and round, made of wood and covered with hide.

Prepared cardboard grips on supports, stapled to shield.

Angel's wings

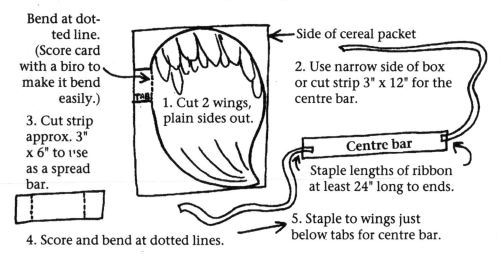

Bend at dotted line. (Score card with a biro to make it bend easily.)

3. Cut strip approx. 3" x 6" to use as a spread bar.

4. Score and bend at dotted lines.

Side of cereal packet

2. Use narrow side of box or cut strip 3" x 12" for the centre bar.

1. Cut 2 wings, plain sides out.

Centre bar

Staple lengths of ribbon at least 24" long to ends.

5. Staple to wings just below tabs for centre bar.

6. Staple wing tabs to centre bar at a slight angle, about 4" apart.

7. Cover with foil.

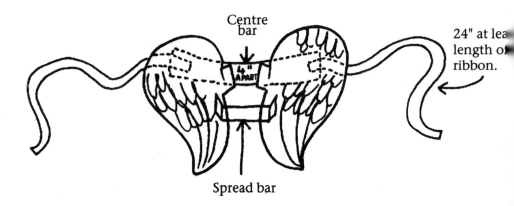

Centre bar

24" at least length of ribbon.

Spread bar

Tip Leave wing foil plain or draw in feather shapes with black marker.

NB Remember to staple spread bar to wings before stapling wings to centre bar. If done the other way, it is very difficult to staple the spread bar.

Angel's Wings II

1. Cut out two wings as before.
2. Cut out centre bar as before and attach ribbons.
3. Staple wings to bar to lie flat across the back.

To attach wings

Ideally, halo should sit on head like the brim of a hat, but you may attach a ribbon and tie it if necessary.

Ribbons from centre bar are brought from under child's arms to front, crossed and taken back up over the shoulders. They can be tied behind the neck or at the centre bar.

3. Footwear

In most cases, the children will wear their own clothes under their costumes. On special occasions, where they want to be fully engaged in their parts, they might go bare-foot or wear:

* sandals on bare feet
* ballet shoes with the ribbon criss-crossed up to the knee
* Black runners/sneakers with black ribbon criss-crossed up to the knee.

The illustrations on pages 20-23 offer a series of possibilities for various types of character.

CHAPTER 3

Making and Using Props

The most effective prop at your disposal will be the imagination of your audience. Use it to the full. A few well chosen words before a performance will set the scene in the minds of the congregation.

Elaborate props will not be necessary – existing church furniture can be converted for your use. For example, a table turned on its side makes a screen for the humans behind the hand puppets.

Cardboard boxes, redesigned, covered or painted, make chariots, houses, walls, tables, donkey's heads and boats. Once the children dress up for their parts, the particular scene is set by adding some appropriate implements, for example, a carpenter's workshop comes alive when the children pretend to saw a length of wood placed between two chairs. A bale of hay, a length of rope and some garden tools help to give an image of field or vineyard workers. A market setting may be created by upturned boxes covered with cloth and laid with a variety of colourful items for sale, and some children sitting cross-legged at their stalls while potential customers wander around looking and bargaining.

Cover a table or upturned box with a white cloth and place on it a wooden bowl with fruit, a loaf of bread, some cheese and drinking vessels for a meal, the setting for many scripture stories.

A covered table with a scroll placed in the centre, and a benediction candelabra or candlestick with lighting candles, gives an atmosphere of Temple or synagogue.

Lanterns for the wise and foolish virgins may be made from folded paper or from empty wine cartons with windows cut in the sides (see diagrams on page 27). Coloured cellophane paper pasted to the insides of the windows gives a pleasant glow when a battery torch is placed inside.

Lanterns

A: A simple paper lantern

1. Take a sheet of A4 paper and fold lengthwise.

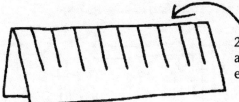

2. Make 2" - 3" slits along the folded edge.

3. Unfold and bend the other way to make a tube.

4. Slightly press the two ends together to help the slits to open. If they do not open, you may need to lengthen the slits.

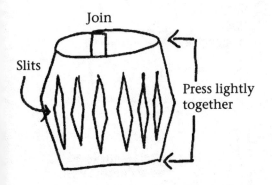

Join

Slits

Press lightly together

5. Glue or sellotape on the handle.

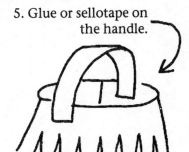

B: Lantern from empty wine carton

1. Cut out windows from two or four sides.

2. From the inside, cover with yellow or red cellophane.

3. Paint or cover the outside with black paper.

A life-sized cross made from large cereal packets will be very light for a child to carry. Staple or tape the boxes securely end to end and cover with brown paper. You will need seven same-sized cereal packets, some wide sellotape, a stapler, and sheets of brown wrapping paper. Open both ends of the boxes, and place one flap inside the other.

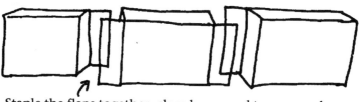

Staple the flaps together, close boxes and tape securely. These form the cross-bar.

From the middle box, attach one box above and three below, using the same means to attach them.

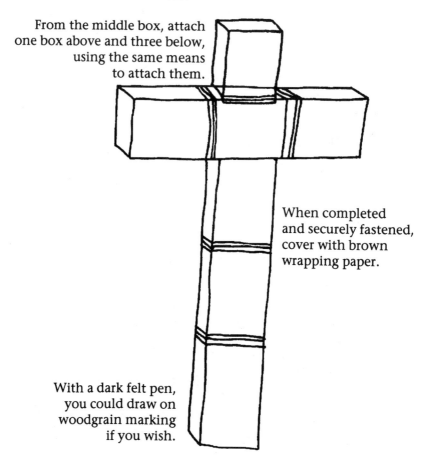

When completed and securely fastened, cover with brown wrapping paper.

With a dark felt pen, you could draw on woodgrain marking if you wish.

A river or lake could be a length of blue cloth placed on the floor with a child at each end causing it to ripple gently. Garden net serves as a fishing net and fish are made by cutting out cardboard shapes. Scripture messages might be written on the fish and the children can fish them out of the river or lake with a stick, line and hook. The fish should have a cotton or nylon loop taped at the mouth for the hook to catch. The shape of the fish can be adapted as necessary but the dimensions should be about 8" long by 5-6" wide.

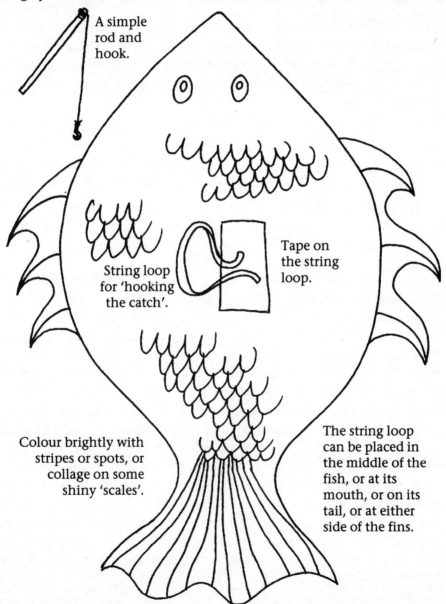

A simple rod and hook.

String loop for 'hooking the catch'.

Tape on the string loop.

Colour brightly with stripes or spots, or collage on some shiny 'scales'.

The string loop can be placed in the middle of the fish, or at its mouth, or on its tail, or at either side of the fins.

Another idea would be to hand the fish out to the children first and ask them to put their names on them. Put all the fish in the river and ask the children to fish one out. The child will then be asked to remember in her/his prayers during the week the child whose name is on the fish s/he caught.

A foldable wooden frame or screen, about six feet high and twelve feet wide, made in two sections and hinged together, would be useful to hang backdrops, paintings, drawings and to use as a screen.

Bundles of dried grasses are good for outdoor scenes such as the harvest stories, disciples eating ears of corn on the Sabbath, etc. Ask the children and their families to collect grasses when they are out walking in the summer. Tie them in bundles and hang them upside down in a warm, airy place to dry.

Children are just as sentimental as adults and if you keep props in storage for next year the children will delight in recounting their memories when those old props are brought out for use again. They may want them used in exactly the same way as before, just as they like the same story to be told over and over again.

Easter Garden

A very beautiful Easter Garden can be built on a fairly large scale without much difficulty and the children will enjoy bringing in items for it. One or two adults would need to take responsibility for co-ordinating the project, to control what comes in and to label items on loan, ensuring that they are returned to the rightful owners. Choose a suitable place in your church or hall, against a wall or in a corner. Place a waterproof sheet on the floor as a base for the garden and cover with sand, pebbles or moss. Build a tomb with a cardboard box covered and lined with grey cloth or plastic to resemble stone. Strong grey or black paper might also be used for the tomb but it may get damp when the garden is being watered. Decorate the tomb with moss or ivy and the garden with potted plants, flowers and shrubs. You may be lucky enough to borrow a miniature fountain or waterfall suitable for indoors. If not, use a piece of mirror for a lake or pond. To this garden can be added a wide variety of butterflys, birds, animals and people. See chapter 6, on sculpture, for ideas on making figures for your Easter Garden, such as the women who saw where Jesus was laid to rest on Good Friday and the women who went to anoint him on the morning after the Sabbath, the figure of Jesus laid in the tomb covered with a white cloth and the figure of Jesus whom Mary Magdalen thought was the gardener. Angels, soldiers and bystanders can also be added with a shepherd and some sheep (see diagram in chapter 11).

The Jesse Tree

You may wish to have a Jesse tree during the Advent Season, celebrating the ancestory of Jesus. It is usually an evergreen tree with symbols hanging from its branches.

The name 'Jesse' comes from Jesse, the father of king David, and Jesus is of the line of David, as the bible tells us. The Jesse tree represents the royal 'family tree' of Jesus, (Mt 1:1-17) and shows his 'roots'. The image of the tree is taken from Isaiah 11:1, 'A shoot shall sprout from the stump of Jesse, and from his roots a bud shall blossom.' The shoot is traditionally regarded as Mary, and Jesus as the blossom.

The tree is also symbolic of the Tree of Life. It began to appear in German art and books in the eleventh century and then appeared throughout Europe in stained glass, sculpture and manuscripts. The Jesse Tree itself is a modern development, designed in 1949 by an American nun. It is a symbol of joyful expectation, the true meaning of Advent as we await the coming of our Saviour at Christmas. Symbols like the Jesse tree can help our reflections while waiting for Christmas. The symbols to be hung on the tree can be made from any material. The most successful we ever made were cut from thin white card, drawn on with thick black felt pen. The white and black against the green tree was most effective.

The tree is placed in the sanctuary after the 8th of December. Stress that it is not a Christmas tree, so it should not have lights, glitter or coloured balls 'decorating' it. Some symbols can be placed on the tree each Sunday, with perhaps a card beside the tree explaining each symbol, with its scriptural text or reference beside it for the benefit of the congregation. We list some examples of appropriate symbols on the next page.

Symbols

Triangle – relates to the Godhead of Jesus.

Square – signifies Christ is the cornerstone.

Circle – life without end

Sun, moon, stars – Creation

Serpent and fruit – promise to Adam and Eve (Gen 3)

Ark or Rainbow – promise to Noah (Gen 6)

Ram – promise to Abraham (Gen 12, 15)

Sceptre – promise to Judah (Gen 49)

Lion – of Judah (Gen 49)

Coat of colours – Joseph, type of Christ (Gen 37)

Tablets of Law – Moses (Deut 18)

Star of David – prophecy of David (Ps 109)

Hand – (Is 6)

Cloud – prophecy of Isaiah (Is 45:8)

Cross – prophecies of Jeremiah (Jer 11)

Broken chain – prophecies of Ezekiel (Ezek 34, 37)

Whale – Jonah – a figure of Christ (Jon 2)

Altar – prophecy of Malachi. (Mal 1)

*The last seven are linked with the 'O' antiphons.

Hour Glass – prophecy of Daniel 'O Sapientia' (Dan 19)

Silhouette of Bethlehem – prophecy of Micheas 'O Adonis' (Mich 5)

Shell – John the Baptist 'O Radix Jesse' (Is 40)

Lamb of God – John the Baptist 'O Clavis David' (Mal 3, Jn 1)

Carpenter's Square – St Joseph 'O Oriens'

Crown of Twelve Stars – Mary, Mother of Christ 'O Rex Gentium' (Rev 12)

Chi-Rho – Christ our Saviour 'O Emmanuel' (Lk 2:1-14)

Other Christian symbols: the Fish, Alpha, Omega, King's crown, Wheat, Grapes, White Dove.

Biblical words: Love, Joy, Hope, Peace, Stars.

These symbols could be put on the tree on Christmas Eve

The Jesse Tree

The children can help draw and cut out the symbols while learning about their meaning.

Chi-Ro

Evergreen tree is best, if possible.

The base itself is a triangle. A bucket is easier and more practical for most people.

Notes on props:

CHAPTER 4

Making and Using Puppets

Puppets have a long pedigree in the field of entertainment and they do get the message across. From *Punch and Judy* to modern TV shows like *Sesame Street* and *Fraggle Rock,* children are captivated by the small characters as they unfold a story.

And characters are what they are. Puppets very quickly and easily inhabit the role assigned to them, while adding a magic of their own. Whether it is one puppet character reading a story, or a number of them performing a piece, it is a good way to gain children's attention and interest in presenting a story or theme. With a group of twelve-year-olds, we have made puppets, and have written and performed the themes. We made and used glove puppets as these were the easiest to make and operate.

You will need some kind of screen behind which the puppet operators sit. A table turned on its side might be adequate, with the puppeteers wearing unobtrusive clothing. Puppeteers must remember to hold the puppets high above the table edge, to be seen. The readers can use different voices for the various characters, or simply narrate.

The story of Moses in the bullrushes is a suitable storyline for puppets to develop. The characters can be made from socks or made up as glove puppets. If you choose to use socks as the basis of your puppets, the characterisation will be more along the lines of *Kermit* and *Fraggle Rock,* with the emphasis on the head and mouth. You lose out on arm movement, but there might be stories in which this is not so important.

With the glove puppet, there is the advantage of a more 'human' representation, with an emphasis on their body reactions to each other rather than concentrating on the head and mouth.

The diagram for the glove puppet, is in the right proportions but you should check the size of the hand which it has to fit before cutting it out. It is made in a 'Y' shape to facilitate operating the puppet. We made the gloves from old sheeting or pillowcase material, then 'dressed' them as befitted the character needed.

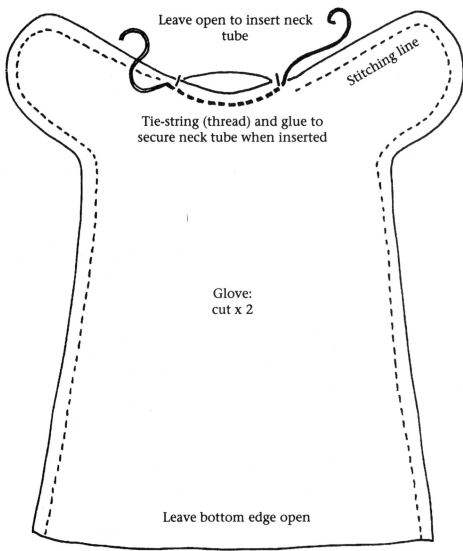

Leave open to insert neck tube

Stitching line

Tie-string (thread) and glue to secure neck tube when inserted

Glove:
cut x 2

Leave bottom edge open

This basic glove pattern can be adapted for size as necessary

The head is made from a sheet of newspaper screwed up into a loose ball, the approximate size of a tennis ball. Make a hole with your finger at one end where the neck will be, and insert a cardboard tube large enough to take your forefinger. Tape on and secure with pasted paper strips.

As with the papier maché for the sculpted figures (see chapter 5), you will need newspapers and wallpaper paste, and some empty jam jars. The cardboard for the neck tube can be taken from an empty cereal box.

Tear strips of newspaper 1"-2" wide, paste up and wind around the base like an Egyptian Mummy, including the neck tube inserted earlier.

After the head has begun to take shape, add small wads of pasted newspaper to build up the nose and chin, if desired. The head can also be left as a round ball, (which is simpler).

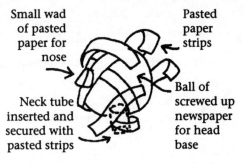

Small wad of pasted paper for nose

Pasted paper strips

Neck tube inserted and secured with pasted strips

Ball of screwed up newspaper for head base

Place the completed head on a jam jar to dry. If it can be left in the airing cupboard or a warm, dry place, it facilitates the drying process.

Having made up the 'glove', take the dried head and paint as required. Remember that clean bright colours will show more clearly than soft understated colouring.

Hair (for those without veils) can be made most easily from wool, the very thick kind is best. If the character doesn't need long hair, carpet wool is excellent. The hair can be any colour, as the important thing is that the puppet can be clearly seen. Start from the lowest level and work up.

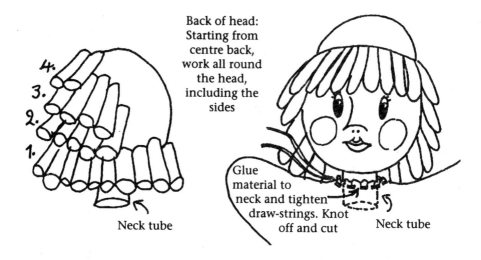

To attach the head to the glove, insert the neck tube into the neck opening on the glove, and spread a line of glue where the material meets the cardboard tube. Pull the drawstrings to hold the material in place closely against the tube, check that it is sticking and leave to dry.

Dressing the Puppets

Remember that only the top half of the puppets can be seen, so concentrate on their heads and trunks to give individuality and character. Useful pieces of clothing include tabards, waistcoats, shoulder/waist sashes, veils, head-cloths, turbans, skull-caps, beards, cloaks, shawls, neckerchiefs, brooches, and ear-rings, and details such as buttons and pockets.

Sock Puppets
Presenting the sock puppets can be done in the same way as the hand puppets, from behind a table. Because they are, in many ways, more intimate characters than the glove puppets, they could also simply sit on their animator's knee and carry on a conversation or dialogue with other puppets or humans from there.

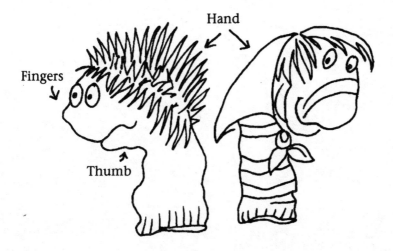

You will need socks – all sorts, plain, stripped etc. There are often odd ones of a pair lying around! Wool or fur for hair, red felt or material for mouths and lips, a variety of bought and made up eyes, including the kind that 'swivel' when the head is moved.

Put the sock on your hand to see where the mouth, eyes and hair all need to go. The mouth moves by moving and bunching your fingers and hand, so roughly the mouth will be at the 'toe' of the sock, the eyes on top, made visible when your hand is 'bunched'. The best way is to try it out and see for yourself.

Like the hand puppets, making them move is very important. Your hand, wrist, fingers and forearm can all be utilised to great effect in both kinds of puppets.

Once again, the best way is to try it and see for yourself – and they are fun to practice!

These 'sock' characters are very good at showing emotion, so could be used to more advantage in a dialogue situation that is making some 'moral' point, e.g., it might be the disadvantages of stealing, lying, cheating etc., or the advantages of being kind, helpful, or making the best out of difficult situations.

Notes on Puppets:

CHAPTER 5

Sculpture and Tableau-Making

Tableaux as aids for liturgical focus
For certain times in the liturgical year, a tableau illustrating an aspect of the event is very effective. A tableau is a group of figures representing or portraying an event: a living picture. In mimed tableau, people 'freeze' into the required positions to heighten the dramatic effect of the scene they are representing. In the present context, I mean sculpted or modelled figures. A well-known example is the traditional nativity scene at Christmas time, with the baby brought in procession and placed in the crib during the main Christmas service or the children's service, and the kings making their appearance at Epiphany.

Another appropriate time is Lent. On several occasions in school, we have based a Lenten tableau on various Stations of the Cross. (These are scenes showing Jesus' journey to Calvary with his cross, beginning with Pilate washing his hands. They are a traditional feature around the walls of a Roman Catholic church.) Sometimes we have let these scenes stand in their own right as depicting Christ's journey to Calvary, changing the Station two or three times during the seven-week Lenten period. At other times we have expanded this theme to incorporate a suitable topical theme. It could be linked to an issue of justice, peace, exploitation, violence or reconciliation, for example. These areas might help the children's awareness (and our own) of the problems faced by many people in the world today, linking them with the same problems faced by the people of Jesus' time. Another idea might be to link the tableau with something the children are following in RE classes. Or again it might usefully be linked with our personal journey in the awareness of God's love for us.

The figures we made and used were approximately two to three feet high, made of chicken wire and papier maché. If simply designed and constructed, children of all ages enjoy helping to make them with adult help and supervision. Although we made simple male/female figures, no-one was specifically anyone in particular. This meant they could become interchangeable, which can be interesting if showing Simon of Cyrene helping Jesus with his cross. Who is Simon, who is Jesus? Ask the children. Everyone has their own reasons for choosing a particular figure, but interchangability also says something in our lives too. Sometimes we need help, and sometimes we can give help. The figures can be made as specific or not as desired. We painted ours with a bronze finish, which gave the effect of bronze sculpture. They could also be painted naturalistically or material could be swathed around them to give a more realistic effect of the clothing of the times.

To make the armature

You will need some pieces of chicken wire, a pair of wire cutters, and some gardening gloves to protect your hands. Follow the steps in the following diagrams, depending on which shapes you decide you want to make. The simplest body shape to make is the cone: Cut and bend a piece of chicken wire into the shape. (Sizes are approximate).

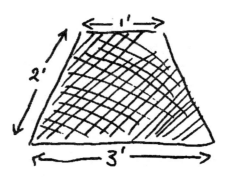

Top end

Use the loose clipped wire ends to fasten the struture together.

Check that it stands firmly.

Bottom end

Cut and bend a second piece of chicen wire into a tube x 2

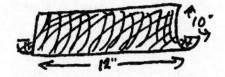

These tubes will be the arms, so flatten the ends for hands.

Attach the arms to the sides of the cone structure, near the top.

Use loose wire ends to attach the arms to the body

For the head, you can make an egg-shape from chicken wire *or* use an inflated balloon, (careful it doesn't burst!) Attach the head to the narrow neck end of the cone.

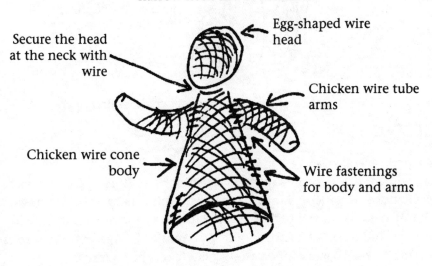

Secure the head at the neck with wire

Egg-shaped wire head

Chicken wire tube arms

Chicken wire cone body

Wire fastenings for body and arms

Now you are ready to start the papier maché process

More body-shaped armatures

The cone body shape can be a little uninteresting if used exclusively, so it is good to use different kinds of shapes for the trunk. Rectangles or tubes are also versatile body shapes. Chicken wire tubes can be made longer, stronger and thicker to make legs. Make sure the feet are large enough and strong enough to support the figure, and that the figure itself is well balanced enough to stand alone.

In a Lenten tableau, various figures could carry spears or whips. Veronica would be holding her cloth.

Head tube, ends closed and sides pulled out to make a circular shape

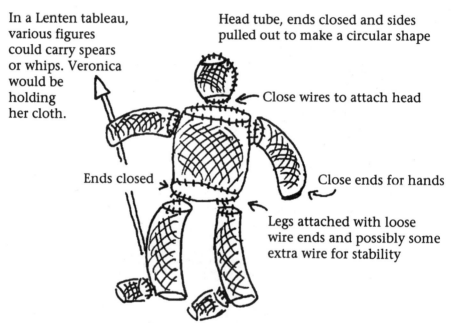

Close wires to attach head

Ends closed

Close ends for hands

Legs attached with loose wire ends and possibly some extra wire for stability

Close the ends of the legs – the feet could be left open

To make papier maché

You will need lots of newspapers, a packet of wallpaper paste, a large plastic bowl in which to mix up the paste (mix the paste according to the instructions on the packet), some brushes to put the paste on with, or you could use your hands. Aprons, overalls or a large unwanted shirt of Dad's to keep some of the paste/water etc off the children.

Strips of newspaper, approximately 6" x 12" and well pasted, are wound round 'mummy' fashion to build up the figure

An example of a cone figure: Veronica and her cloth:

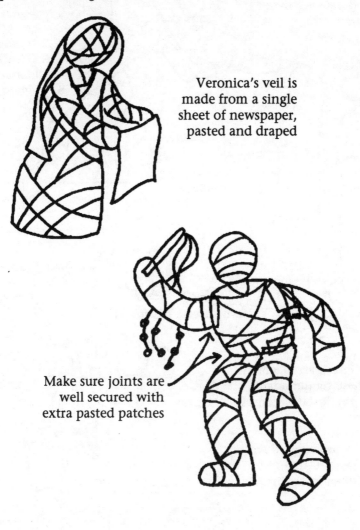

Veronica's veil is made from a single sheet of newspaper, pasted and draped

Make sure joints are well secured with extra pasted patches

Lent sculpture tableau

The figures should be made stable enough to stand on their own

These figures were 'bronzed'

Boxes of different heights and covered with cloth or blankets form a good platform for the tableau

Jesus meets his mother

A different arrangement of these figures adapts into the Risen Christ of Easter.

This could be used with the Easter Garden described in chapter 3.

CHAPTER 6

Using an Overhead Projector

The overhead projector can benefit your work in preparing and delivering children's liturgy in a number of ways. It can be used to display hymns and songs with which the congregation are not familiar. The telling of a story may be enhanced by displaying drawings to illustrate the theme. A picture might be revealed bit by bit as the story is told.

Your material may be written, drawn free-hand or photocopied on to an acetate (the clear cellophane sheets used in the projector). The picture may be black and white or in colour.

While ensuring you are not breaking copyright laws, a drawing can be copied on to acetate, transferred on to a large sheet of cloth or paper pinned to a wall, and the image captured by drawing or painting it. It can also be projected onto a bare wall or a window (see stained glass section).

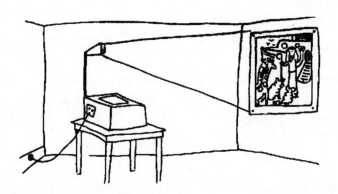

These drawings/paintings can be used for backdrops to a drama or mime. They might be displayed around the walls of the church or hall in the form of a frieze telling a story in sequence over a number of weeks. For example, the series of appearances Jesus made to various people between his death and his Ascension into heaven, or the series of events from the annunciation to Jesus' birth.

Reproduce a drawing on to a window pane by placing sheets of white paper or cloth behind the glass to be painted. Project your picture, which you have first drawn on an acetate, on to the sheet through the glass. Outline the picture with a fine paintbrush, using poster paints, onto the glass. The paints or markers used should be washable for removing afterwards. Paint in the picture. Children of ten years and over will be well able to do this task under adult supervision.

Some hints
• Write in good sized legible print.

• Cover only one or two items or points per acetate.

• Use coloured markers to highlight words and make pictures cheerful and interesting. Ensure the picture is in clear focus, and take care not to let any part of your body come between the lens and the screen, especially if you have your back to the screen when using the overhead projector.

• Position the screen close to the main altar as this allows the congregation to see the screen and the celebrant without distraction.

• Switch off the machine when you have finished with an acetate, as it becomes a distraction.

•

It is not advisable to use the overhead projector every week as it can dull your incentive to use other visual images and become boring for the congregation.

Overcoming problems
The design of your church or hall might be such that when you have the overhead projector to one side of the main altar some people sitting at the side may not be able to see it. In time, given the space, these people will move to the centre of their own accord. If the space is not available for them to move, then it will be important to think again about the value of this medium in these circumstances.

Stained glass window

If you don't want to paint directly on to the windows, it is possible to make stained glass windows out of coloured cellophane, or tissue paper and black paper. These can be blu-taked or pinned to existing window frames, allowing the light to shine through.

Alternatively, they could be attached to a frame and a light placed behind it for illumination.

The design can be abstract or figurative. Remember that stylised shapes are easier to work on than naturalistic shapes. Ensure that the design cut out of the black backing paper leaves plenty of paper to connect the image and keep it fom falling apart.

 A

1. Measure a 2-3" margin around the black paper.

2. With white chalk, draw the layout of the design (A).

3. When you're happy with design, re-draw it carefully, remembering to leave the black paper outline intact to hold the picture together.

 B

4. Cut away parts to be filled with color, using a craft knife. It will look a bit like a stencil (B).

C

5. Reverse black paper frame-work (which is the 'leading' of your picture) and stick coloured cellophane or tissue on the back (C).

6. When the glue is thoroughly dried, pin to a window.

7. If the window is large, several pictures telling a story, such as 'creation-Genesis', or making an abstract design, could be arranged on the one window (D).

D
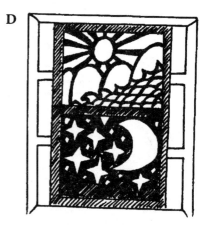

Stained glass window illumination frame

A two, three or four-sided light wooden frame of the size you require can be made simpy from cheap wood, along the lines of the old clothes horse.

Light wooden battens

Material
hinge
Tacked on *inside* the frame works best

The stained glass designs are stuck or pinned onto the framework, and a shaded light bulb, to diffuse the light, of appropriate low wattage, is placed inside.

NB: Make sure the light is not too close to the paper or cellophane at any point.

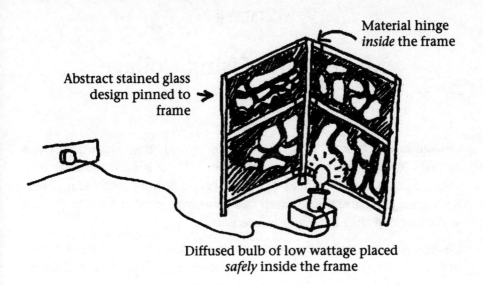

Material hinge *inside* the frame

Abstract stained glass design pinned to frame ➔

Diffused bulb of low wattage placed *safely* inside the frame

Notes on overhead projectors

CHAPTER 7

Making and Using Collage

Collage is a technique of picture-making by applying paper, magazine cuttings, cloth, feathers, paint and other non-perishable material to a sheet of paper, card or canvas. It is a very good technique to use in children's liturgy because the children can contribute materials to the picture and know that they have participated.

Collage pictures can be figurative, where the core of the picture is drawn or painted on a large sheet and other materials stuck on by the children to complete the scene. For example, paint sky, mountains and some earth-coloured foreground and then allow the children to stick on houses, people, sheep trees and birds.

For themes such as challenge, justice, peace, reconciliation, the children can bring in cuttings from magazines and newspapers, drawings, words written on paper shapes, postcards, photographs, etc., which they feel are relevant to the topic, and they can stick them on a large sheet of paper or card hung up for this purpose.

Footprints, or paving stones cut from card, may be used to make a collage directly on to a wall or floor depicting a journey or way to travel, for example, the way of the cross at Easter. For themes encouraging us to follow Jesus' footsteps and to depict journeys such as the flight of the Israelites out of Egypt or the journey into the promised land, the collage can be built up over a number of weeks (see diagram opposite).

A prayer collage

Give the children plain or shaped pieces of card – butterflies, flowers, hands, hearts, etc. Ask them to make up a prayer and write it on the card, if necessary with the help of an adult. Colour the cards and stick the completed cards on a sheet of paper at random or in a pattern. Make a prayer garden or a prayer tree, depending on which shapes you decide to use. They could also be blu-taked directly on to a wall or screen. Once you begin thinking about it, you will have lots of your own ideas.

Ask the children to bring in photographs of themselves which they don't mind parting with and, when making a collage with children in it, use the faces of children cut from the photos for the children in the collage. This idea can be used when making a collage of Jesus gathering the children around him. It has a magic effect on the children as it makes it so personal for them.

Collage

Children and adults contribute 'live' footprints for this collaged analogy of our life's journey with the Israelites' journey into the Promised Land.

Liturgy Board

Collage can also be used to make a 'Liturgy Board'. The use of a liturgy board can focus a theme, especially the more abstract ideas, and help to reinforce the message, not only for the children who can contribute to its making, but also for adults in the congregation.

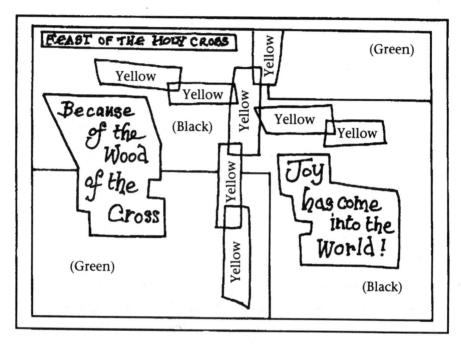

Coloured sheets make up the background. The cross is put together in a contrasting colour (in this case yellow), and the lettering is black on white. Choose your own colours. The colours of the liturgical season could be a guide.

Notes on collage:

CHAPTER 8

Making and Using Banners

Banners make very good 'focusing' points, especially if eye-catching, carrying the theme out to the congregation, or helping to consolidate what they have just heard or seen.

They can be made simply, cheaply and quickly using a paper collage method. More enduring ones can be made in fabrics. Quite a good way is to make banners for the liturgical season, such as Advent, Christmas, Lent, Easter, Pentecost, etc., in fabric, and others of a more topical nature from collaged paper and card throughout the year.

If you are making a banner for a particular space, e.g. in front of the lectern, you will need to measure the space first.

Collaged banners

If you have a local printing works, it could be a good source of large coloured sheets of card, at not too great a cost, which are a more substantial backing than paper. You could also use it to make up a card and paper template to see what a particular design would look like before making it up in fabrics.

You will need sheets of coloured and white card approximately 20" x 25", a roll of wide sellotape or any wide sticky tape, scissors, pencil, rubber, thick black and coloured felt pen, ruler and tape measure, blu-tak and glue.

For a simple wall banner:
1. Place two sheets of the same colour card end to end and join with sticky tape.
2. Lightly rule a margin approximately 2" in from the edge all round.
3. Choose a simple, effective few words to fit in with the particular theme and emphasis you have chosen to take in your celebration.
4. The simplest way is to write them boldly in black felt pen on white

card or a contrasting colour card, for example, 'Come Holy Spirit' or
'Come Spirit of Life' for Pentecost. Remember to write large enough.

5. Cut around the words rather than each individual letter, which in
itself makes an interesting design shape against the backing sheet.
Sometimes it is effective to cut out the individual letters (see diagrams).

6. Spend a bit of time arranging the letters and words in a lively, eye-
catching design, sticking with blu-tak and hanging up if necessary to see
how it looks before the final sticking down with glue.

7. You could also include a simple, appropriate motif behind the lettering.

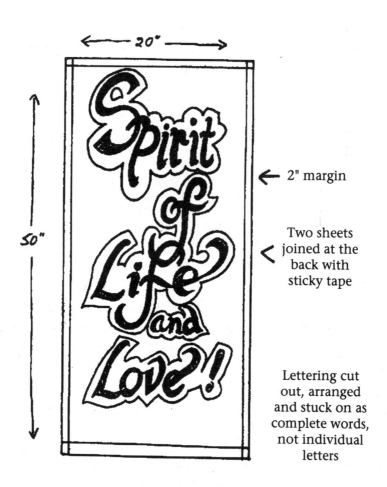

Simple motif of a
dove for the Holy
Spirit →

2" margin ──→

Two sheets
joined at the ⟩
back with
sticky tape

A good way of strengthening the edges is to stick tape all along the
edges on the reverse side of the banner. In any case, stick some on the
backs of the corners. It lessens the damage done by blu-tak when taking
down the banner.

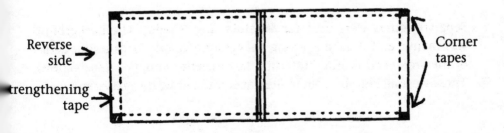

Reverse →
side

Corner
tapes

strengthening →
tape

Easter collage banners

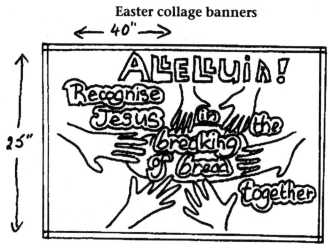

In this banner, children and adults drew around their own hands in pencil. These were overdrawn in black felt pen, as was the lettering and bread, then cut out and stuck on. The back sheets were in two colours, one green and one yellow, placed side by side.

Separate letters were used for 'Alleluia' and 'Credo'. The background was mauve and it gave a strong background colour for the silhouettes of the broken cross and butterflies (an ancient symbol of resurrection). These were all cut out from white paper and left white against mauve.

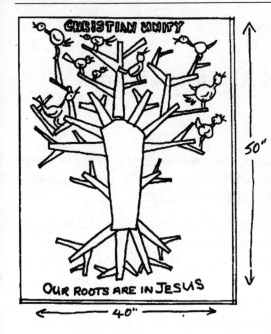

CHRISTIAN UNITY

OUR ROOTS ARE IN JESUS

50"

40"

The Family Tree of Christian Unity is something children love contributing to by way of sticking on branches (built up from strips of white paper) or by making birds to sit on the branches. Names of various churches or denominations could be written on the various branches. This one was made on a background of two different coloured sheets of card.

You can make a larger banner by using four or six sheets instead of two. You could also use different coloured backing sheets.

Fabric banners

All the ideas suggested for the collage banners can be adapted to make fabric banners if desired. It is best to look around fabric shops for remnants that would be suitable to make up into banners, as felt is now very expensive.

The simplest method to make a banner from fabric is appliqué, which is the fabric equivalent of collage. Again, keep shapes and lettering simple, colourful and clear. A heavier, plain fabric is more suitable for the backcloth. Almost anything can be appliquéd on to this.

There are several books available on making liturgical banners, most of them rather specialised. A combination of your own ideas and sewing skills, plus some of their basic suggestions could be helpful to you.

Remember that you might have to weight the bottom, and hang them from something rigid like a dowelling rod.

CHAPTER 9

Themes and Abstract Themes

The readings for the Sunday liturgy follow a three-year cycle. We have listed, in chapter 12, the first two readings and the gospel for each Sunday of the three years of the Roman Lectionary.

We usually pick the theme for the liturgy from the gospel and first reading, which normally link into each other. On occasions we have found that the main theme is not concrete enough to get the message across to the children in the short time available, and have picked the theme from the second reading instead.

Often one theme stands out from the readings of the day and sometimes several themes present themselves and you have to choose. In our list of readings we have given you one or two themes for each gospel.

When preparing children's liturgy, you will need to read the three readings, choose a theme and then decide on your presentation. In our listings in chapter 12, we refer you to chapters in this book which we think you might find helpful for each Sunday. The needs of each liturgy group will, of course, be different and our aim is not to swamp you with our ideas but to help you tap into your own resources.

Some themes are quite abstract and do not lend themselves to mime, puppetry etc. In these cases, you may be able to use imagery such as in the gospel of the 18th Sunday of Year B, Jn 6:24-35: 'I am the bread of life.' Ask the children what food is needed for the body. Prepare a collage of a family around a meal table or have some food such as bread, fruit, water etc., on a table to remind the children of earthly food. Then talk about food for the soul, love, kindness, sensitivity, helpfulness, prayerfulness, praise of God, etc., and prepare a collage using magazine cut-outs or drawings to demonstrate the different types of nourishment for the soul. Talk about how it feels for them to give and to receive food for the soul.

Another example occurs on the 21st Sunday of Year C: Lk 13:22-30: 'Try your best to enter by the narrow door'. This one could be dealt with in terms of friendship. Different levels of friendship in the child's life, someone I know to see but not to speak to, someone I say 'hello!' to, my classmate, my neighbour, my best friend. Who would I invite to my party or to stay over at my house? Who do you think Jesus would invite to stay over at his house? What must we do to be Jesus' friend?

Give the children circles of card and ask them to draw their own faces. Stick these around a picture of Jesus who is welcoming them into his house.

Are there people who might choose not to go to Jesus' house?

Keep notes from year to year, especially if the presentation was well received, as you may not remember when the same theme comes up again.

Notes:

CHAPTER 10

Working with Hymns and Songs

Singing is a very important part of any celebration. In some Christian traditions hymn singing plays a well-established part in the service and in others the congregation has to be coaxed to sing. In the case of the latter, there is no hope at all of getting them to sing unless the tunes are familiar and the words are provided for them.

Since we are concerned in this book with visual aids, let us look at some of the ways you can provide your congregation with the words of the hymns/songs.

Start with a small selection of familiar hymns to cover the sequence or format of the service, e.g. entrance, offertory, communion, recessional, as in the Roman Catholic and Anglican liturgies. Type these on two sides of an A4 sheet of paper, photocopy the required number and slide them into clear plastic covers to be handed out to the people before the service, and collected afterwards. We have seen up to twenty-four hymns printed on one A4 sheet quite legibly.

Number the hymns/songs for easy access.

Sing the same hymns/songs week after week, dropping one and adding a new one every eight to ten weeks. This gives the congregation time to become familiar with the hymns/songs in the church context. Where services are held a number of times weekly in the school context, the hymns/songs may be changed more frequently.

Another idea is to buy a supply of ring folders and add new pages to them as required, thereby building up a collection of hymns/songs.

You may decide to use one of the many hymns books on the market. In this case you will be restricted to the hymns in that book.

Type or hand write the hymns/songs on sheets of acetate and, with the overhead projector, reproduce the words on a screen (see the chapter on overhead projectors).

It is not advisable to print the words of hymns/songs on a flip chart and stand it in front of the congregation as only the few in front will be able to read it. This method will only work for small groups of twenty to thirty people.

Many hymns/songs are suitable to be sung with actions and the children love this. The Lord's Prayer sung by the children with hand actions helps them to concentrate on the content of the prayer. The children could be invited to stand around the altar with the celebrant to sing the Lord's Prayer.

If your congregation is shy about singing out, plant a few singers among the people throughout the church and let them lead the singing. This sometimes helps.

Notes:

CHAPTER 11

Bringing the message home

It is essential to help children and their parents to see the Word of God received at the Sunday liturgy as an integral part of their lives for that week, not just an isolated event.

In children's liturgies there are many ways of bringing home the message. A drawing relevant to the theme may be photocopied on A4 sheets and handed out at the end of the service for the children to bring home and colour, bringing it back the following week to be displayed on the walls of the church or hall. For themes such as Jesus gathering the children, they could draw and paint a self-portrait which would be hung on the wall surrounding a picture of Jesus. The novelty will wear off if any idea is used too often.

Completed pictures can also be mounted and hung at home or given as presents to parents or grandparents.

Mounting your picture

A simple method is to cut a piece of coloured card about three or four inches larger than the picture to be mounted. Paste the picture on to the centre of the card. Cut a piece of clear contact or cellophane two inches larger than the card and place it on the right side of the picture, clip away excess at corners and fold under at sides. Tape a loop of thread to the back of the picture for hanging (see the diagram opposite).

If the children are old enough to draw their own pictures, let them do so, bearing in mind the visual effectiveness of strong, simple outlines and bright rather than subdued colour.

Smaller children might prefer to colour in a ready-made drawing, which could be drawn by an adult or older child and photocopied. Mounting on coloured card or paper, (which can be obtained from art shops, most stationery shops, or printing works) also helps to give a strong visual impact.

Mounting your pictures

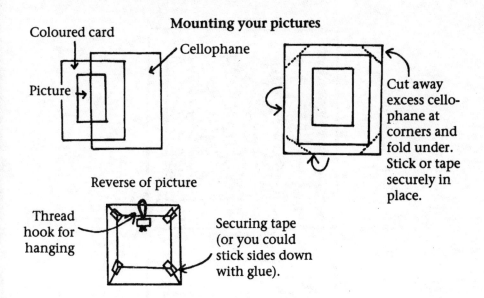

Coloured card

Cellophane

Picture

Cut away excess cellophane at corners and fold under. Stick or tape securely in place.

Reverse of picture

Thread hook for hanging

Securing tape (or you could stick sides down with glue).

Many themes are suitably linked from week to week. To give the children a sense of the life story of Jesus unfolding, it is good to refer back to the previous week and use some of the same visual materials, adding to them as appropriate. If the series of events leading up to Christmas or Easter were painted on large sheets of card or stiff paper, they could be taped together week by week to make a very large picture story book or frieze for the wall.

Frieze on the walls of the church

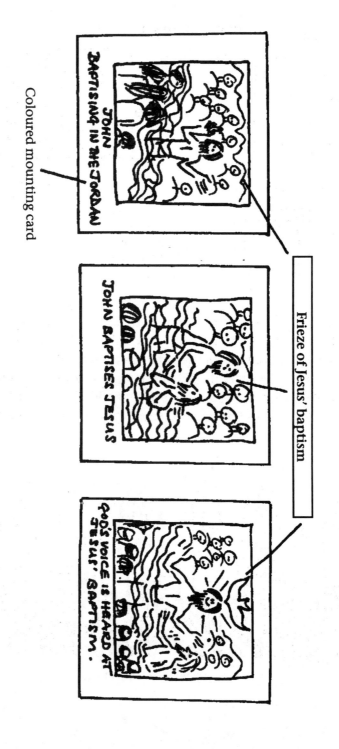

Coloured mounting card

The drawings are done by children or adults and coloured by the children

Frieze of Jesus' baptism

The Christmas story picture book

Annunciation	Visitation	Joseph's dream

Journey to Bethlehem	No room	Birth

and so on with shepherds, kings, flight into Egypt, etc as you require.

For a personal book, these pictures could be mounted and put together as follows:

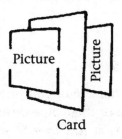

Card

Put one picture on each side of a piece of card. Put the cards in the order you require and then punch each card on the left-hand side. Tie them together with a ribbon.

This could be done on an on-going basis throughout the liturgical year, so that the children would eventually have a picture book of the life of Jesus. For older children, the appropriate scripture references could be included.

Model Desert – Easter Garden

For the weeks covering the story of John the Baptist and Jesus' baptism, the children might like to make a miniature desert.

Materials:
One tea tray
Builders sand or sea sand
Lollypop sticks
Tiny dried or artificial flowers
A small piece of broken mirror
Some stones as big as an adult fist, and some smaller
Small pieces of plain brown, blue or white cloth
White card
Gum or sellotape

Start by filling the tray with sand. Add a cluster of stones for boulders. Sink the mirror in the sand to serve as a pond at an oasis. John might sleep in the shade under the boulders or he might have a tent. Make a tent frame with lollypop sticks, gum and cloth. Next week, to denote a new season, add some flowers to the desert and maybe a tent or two extra. Put up a sign with a lollypop stick and white card. If you are very adventurous, make some people from pipe cleaners and coloured cloth or from plasticine. Camels may be added if the children have them in their play boxes.

Making pipe cleaner people

The size of the pipe cleaner people depends on the size of your model. These are two basic figures made with either two or three pipe cleaners. The smaller one stands at 3" high, the taller one at just over 5" high. Stand them in a piece of playdough or plasticine and 'dress' in scraps of coloured paper or tissue paper. The foil wrappings from sweets are a useful source of gold, silver and coloured decoration or 'jewellery'.

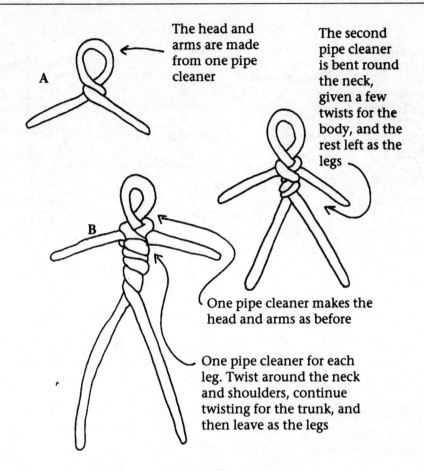

A The head and arms are made from one pipe cleaner

The second pipe cleaner is bent round the neck, given a few twists for the body, and the rest left as the legs

B

One pipe cleaner makes the head and arms as before

One pipe cleaner for each leg. Twist around the neck and shoulders, continue twisting for the trunk, and then leave as the legs

Dressing the pipe cleaner people

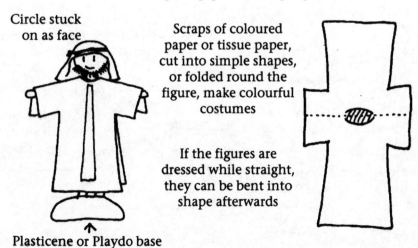

Circle stuck on as face

Scraps of coloured paper or tissue paper, cut into simple shapes, or folded round the figure, make colourful costumes

If the figures are dressed while straight, they can be bent into shape afterwards

Plasticene or Playdo base

Making plasticine people

Head Indent two eyes in a ball of plasticene

Thinly rolled square of plasticene will make hair or head covering

Various body shapes based on the cone or cylinder can be made

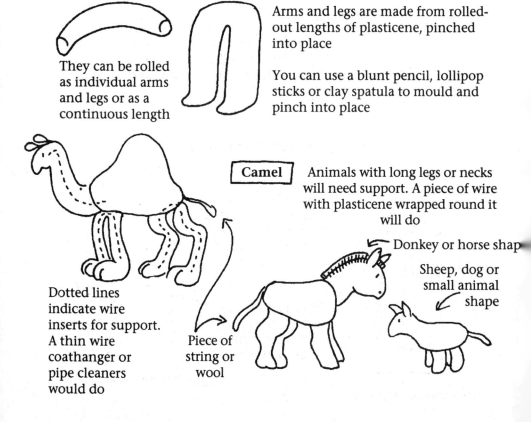

They can be rolled as individual arms and legs or as a continuous length

Arms and legs are made from rolled-out lengths of plasticene, pinched into place

You can use a blunt pencil, lollipop sticks or clay spatula to mould and pinch into place

Camel Animals with long legs or necks will need support. A piece of wire with plasticene wrapped round it will do

Donkey or horse shape

Sheep, dog or small animal shape

Dotted lines indicate wire inserts for support. A thin wire coathanger or pipe cleaners would do

Piece of string or wool

Miniature Easter Garden

A miniature Easter Garden can be made in a similar way.

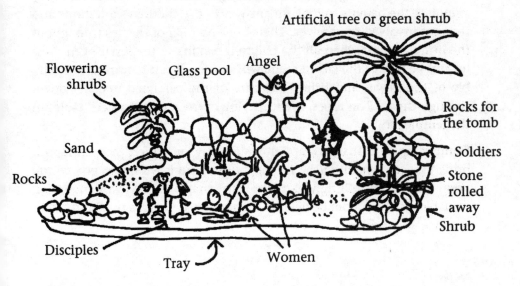

This kind of format could form the basis of your Easter Garden, be it large or small. It could also form the basis of a desert with an oasis by removing the shrubs and adding tents etc.

Another way of getting children to think of the themes at home is to ask them to bring in the raw materials you will need to make visual aids in the coming weeks. Explain to them what the materials will be used for, e.g. empty cereal packets to make a life-sized cross at Easter or to cut hand and foot shapes for themes such as 'helping your neighbour' or 'walking in the path of the Lord'. Excess boxes may be flattened and stored for future use.

Under adult supervision, children might bring in coloured beads, buttons or pebbles for every good deed or act they did during the week. These may be included in the gifts for the offertory procession.

When the children are dressing up for a mime or drama, tell them the story line a week in advance and ask them to practice their part during the week. Ask them to imagine they are living in the days of Jesus. They will bombard their parents and teachers with questions as they spend the week choosing their garments and getting in to the part. This in turn may stimulate the parents to look up answers to the children's questions and thus get involved themselves. There are a number of themes throughout the liturgical year when all the children coming to the service can dress up and be part of the crowd scene without too much rehearsal: the parable of the loaves and fishes, the cure of the paralysed man let down through the roof on ropes, the scattering of the money lenders' tables in the temple etc.

Coming up to Christmas, appoint a Sunday on which each child will bring in a toy which he/she no longer uses and is willing to give to the poor. When they willingly part with a toy that is in good working order, valuable discussion can be held on such topics as generosity, dignity, self-sacrifice and feelings.

Notes:

CHAPTER 12

Themes and Approaches
for each Sunday

We took our themes, or ideas to be illustrated, normally from the gospel reading of the day in the Roman Lectionary. In the third column, we refer to the chapters or approaches in this book which we think are most suitable. We have grouped suggestions for all three Sundays of the cycle together. You may, of course, vary these to suit yourself, but remember that you will begin to lose the interest of the people if you use the same approaches too often.

Readings	Theme	Approaches
Advent:		
1st Sunday		
Year A	The Son of Man is	Mime tableau with
Is 2:1-5.	coming at an hour	narrator, props and
Rom 13:11-14.	you do not expect.	costumes.
Mt 24:37-44.		
		Start Christmas
Year B	Stay awake	story book.
Is 63:16-17, 64:1, 3-8.		
1 Cor 1:3-9.		Begin preparing
Mk 13:33-37.		symbols for Jesse Tree.
Year C	Stay awake	
Jer 33:14-16.		Liturgy board.
1 Thes 3:12-4:2.		
Lk 21:25-28, 34-36.		
2nd Sunday		
Year A	Repent	Repent banner.
Is 11:1-10.	(John the Baptist)	
Rom 15:4-9.		Mime in costume
Mt 3:1-12.		with narrator.

Continued over →

Readings	Theme	Approaches
Year B Is 40:1-5, 9-11. 2 Pet 3:8-14. Mk 1:1-8.	Repent (John the Baptist)	Bringing the message home: Model desert.
Year C Bar 5:1-9. Phil 1:3-6,8-11. Lk 3:1-6.	Make a straight path for the Lord	Liturgy Board. Props: Symbols of baptism.

3rd Sunday

Readings	Theme	Approaches
Year A Is 35:1-6,10. Jas 5:7-10. Mt 11:2-11.	John the Baptist/ Are you the one who is to come?	Drama in costume with props. Assemble Jesse Tree symbols.
Year B Is 61:1-2,10-11. 1 Thes 5:16-24. Jn 1:6-8,19-28.	John baptised with water/Jesus was unknown as yet	Props: Symbols of baptism. Mime with narrator, or drama.
Year C Zeph 3:14-18. Phil 4:4-7. Lk 3:10-18.	What must we do? Share.	Collage a sharing. Mime with narrator.

4th Sunday

Readings	Theme	Approaches
Year A Is 7:10-14. Rom 1:1-7. Mt 1:18-25.	Jesus is born of Mary who was betrothed to Joseph, son of David.	Jesse Tree symbols. Christmas story book.
Year B Sam 7:1-5, 8-11, 16. Rom 16:25-27. Lk 1:26-38.	Annunciation.	Tableau figures of the nativity. Banners. *continued* ➡

continued ➡

Readings	Theme	Approaches
Year C		
Mic 5:1-4.	Mary visits Elizabeth.	Drama or mime.
Heb 10:5-10.		
Lk 1:39-44.		Liturgy board

Season of Christmas

Christmas Day: Dawn Mass	Nativity.	Nativity drama.
Is 62:11-12.		Ideas as above.
Titus 3:4-7.		Liturgy board
Lk 2:15-20.		on light.

Holy Family:		
1st Sunday after Christmas		Wall frieze.
Ecc 3:2-6, 12-14.	Escape to Egypt and	Story book.
Col 3:12-21.	return to Gallilee.	
Year A. Mt 2:13-15, 19-23.		Mime or drama
		with props and
Year B. Lk 2:22-40.	Presentation	costumes.
	in the Temple.	
Year C. Lk 2:41-52.	Jesus is found	
	in the Temple.	

2nd Sunday after Christmas	The Word was made	Abstract Themes:
Ecc 24:1-2, 8-12.	flesh and lived	overhead
Eph 1:3-6, 15-18.	amongst us.	projector.
Jn 1:1-18.		Liturgy board.

Epiphany	Wise men came	Mime or drama.
Is 60:1-6.	to pay homage.	
Eph 3:2-3, 5-6.		Put wise men into
Mt 2:1-12.		nativity scene.

1st Sunday of the Year	Baptism of the Lord.	Symbols of
Is 42:1-4, 6-7.		baptism.
Acts 10:34-38.		
Year A. Mt 3:13-17.		
Year B. Mk 1:7-11.		
Year C. Lk 3:15-16, 21-22.		

Readings	Theme	Approaches
2nd Sunday		
Year A	He is the chosen one of God.	Banners. Abstract themes.
Is 49:3, 5-6. 1 Cor 1:1-3. Jn 1:29-34.		
Year B		
1 Sam 3:3-10, 19. 1 Cor 6:13-15, 17-20. Jn 1:35-42.	We have found the Messiah.	Drama or mime with props.
Year C		
Is 62:1-5. 1 Cor 12:4-11. Jn 2:1-12.	Wedding feast at Cana.	Drama or mime.
3rd Sunday		
Year A		
Is 8:23, 9:3. 1 Cor 1:10-13, 17. Mt 4:12-23.	Jesus leaves Nazareth and chooses apostles. Jesus teaches.	Drama or mime with props and costumes.
Year B		
Jon 3:1-5, 10. 1 Cor 7:29-31. Mk 1:14-20.	Repent and follow me. Choosing apostles.	Banners.
Year C		
Neh 8:2-6, 8-10. 1 Cor 12:12-30. Lk 1:1-4, 4:14-21	Jesus fulfills scripture. Jesus reads in Temple.	Liturgy board.
4th Sunday		
Year A	The Beatitudes.	Simple Collage.
Zeph 2:3, 3:12-13. 1 Cor 1:26-31. Mt 5:1-12.		Banner.

continued →

Readings	Theme	Approaches

Year B
    Deut 18:15-20.
    1 Cor 7:32-35.
    Mk 1:21-28.
	Jesus orders the unclean spirit out of the man. Teaching in the Synagogue.	Drama or mime.

Year C
    Jer 1:4-5, 17-19.
    1 Cor 12:31, 13:13.
    Lk 4:21-30.
	Jesus is not sent to the Jews only. A prophet is not accepted in his own country.	Story telling. Abstract themes: Overhead projector.

5th Sunday

Readings	Theme	Approaches

Year A
    Is 58:7-10.
    1 Cor 2:1-5.
    Mt 5:13-16.
	You are the light of the world. / Love.	Symbols. Liturgy board.

Year B
    Job 7:1-4, 6-7.
    1 Cor 9:16-19, 22-23.
    Mk 1:29-39.
	Jesus heals Simon's mother-in-law and many others.	Mime or drama with costumes.

Year C
    Is 6:1-8.
    1 Cor 15:1-11.
    Lk 5:1-11.
	They filled the boats to sinking point. They left everything and followed him.	Story telling. Props.

6th Sunday

Readings	Theme	Approaches

Year A
    Ecc 15:15-20.
    1 Cor 2:6-10.
    Mt 5:17-37.
	They filled the boats to sinking point. They left everything and followed him.	Abstract themes: Overhead projector.

Year B
    Lev 13:1-2, 45-46.
    1 Cor 10:31, 11:1.
    Mk 1:40-45.
	Jesus cures a leper.	Mime in costume, with narrator.

Year C
    Jer 17:5-8.
    1 Cor 15:12, 16-20.
    Lk 6:17, 20-26.
	Beatitudes.	Collage banners. Puppets with narrator.

The 7th, 8th and 9th Sundays of the year may occur after Easter depending on when Easter falls.

Readings	Theme	Approaches
7th Sunday		

Year A
    Lev 19:1-2, 17-18.
    1 Cor 3:16-23.
    Mt 5:38-48.
	Love your enemies.	Story telling.

Year B
    Is 43:18-19,
        21-22, 24-25.
    2 Cor 1:18-22.
    Mk 2:1-12.
	Jesus forgives sins.
	The cure of the
	paralytic man let
	down through the
	roof.
		Drama or mime
		with narrator.

Year C
    Sam 26:2, 7-9,
        12-13, 22-23.
    1 Cor 15:45-49.
    Lk 6:27-38.
	Compassion.
	Do not judge.
	Your reward is
	in heaven.
		Puppets.

8th Sunday		

Year A
    Is 49:14-15.
    1 Cor 4:1-5.
    Mt 6:24-34.
	Do not worry
	about tomorrow.
		Story telling.

Year B
    Hos 2:16-17, 21-22.
    2 Cor 3:1-6
    Mk 2:18-22.
	Nobody puts new
	wine into old wine
	skins.
	The bridegroom is
	with them.
		Story telling.
		
		Drawings to take
		home.

Year C
    Ecc 27:4-7.
    1 Cor 15:54-58.
    Lk 6:39-45.
	A good man draws
	what is good from
	the store of goodness
	in his heart.
		Story telling.

Readings	Theme	Approaches
9th Sunday		
Year A		
Deut 11:18, 26-28. Rom 3:21-25, 28. Mt 7:21-27.	The house built on rock or built on sand.	Series of drawings in a collage.
Year B		
Deut 5:12-15. 2 Cor 4:6-11. Mk 2:23, 3:6.	Disciples eat ears of corn on the Sabbath.	Drama or mime with costumes and props.
Year C		
Kgs 8:41-43. Gal 1:1-2, 6-10. Lk 7:1-10.	Healing the centurian's servant.	Drama or mime.

Lent

Readings	Theme	Approaches
1st Sunday		
Year A Gen 2:7-9, 3:1-7. Rom 5:12-19. Mt 4:1-11.	Jesus fasts in the wilderness and is tempted.	Start Lent tableau. Make Model Desert and figures.
Year B Gen 9:8-15. 1 Peter 3:18-22. Mk 1:12-15.	Jesus is tempted.	Mime with costumes and props.
Year C Deut 26:4-10. Rom 10:8-13. Lk 4:1-13.	Temptation in the desert.	Liturgy board.
2nd Sunday		
Year A Gen 12:1-4. 2 Tim 1:8-10. Mt 17:1-9.	The Transfiguration.	Lent tableau. Story telling.

continued →

Readings	Theme	Approaches
Year B		
Gen 22:1-2, 9-13, 15-18. Rom 8:31-34. Mk 9:2-10.	The Transfiguration.	Mime with costumes. Drawings to take home.
Year C Gen 15:5-12, 17-18. Phil 3:17, 4:1. Lk 9:28-36.	The Transfiguration.	Liturgy board.
3rd Sunday **Year A** Ex 17:3-7. Rom 5:1-2, 5-8. Jn 4:5-42.	The Samaritan woman at the well.	Mime or drama with costumes and props.
Year B Ex 20:1-17. 1 Cor 1:22-25. Jn 2:13-25.	Jesus drives the money changers from the Temple.	Lent tableau.
Year C Ex 3:1-8, 13-15. 1 Cor 10:1-6, 10-12. Lk 13:1-9.	The fig tree that bore no fruit. Unless your repent you will perish.	Drawings.
4th Sunday **Year A** Sam 16:1, 6-7, 10-13. Eph 5:8-14. Jn 9:1-41.	Jesus heals the blind man.	Bringing the message home. Story telling with costumes and
Year B 2 Chr 36:14-16, 19-23. Eph 2:4-10. Jn 3:14-21.	God sent his son that the world may be saved.	props. Puppets.
Year C Josh 5:9-12. 2 Cor 5:17-21. Lk 15:1-3, 11-32	The prodigal son.	Mime or drama.

Readings	Theme	Approaches
5th Sunday		
Year A	Jesus raises Lazarus	Mime or drama.
Ezek 37:12-14.	from the dead.	
Rom 8:8-11.		
Jn 11:1-45.		
Year B	Jesus faces the reality	Story telling with
Jer 31:31-34.	of his death.	props and
Heb 5:7-9.		costumes.
Jn 12:20-33.		
Year C	The woman caught	Mime or drama.
Is 43:16-21.	in adultery.	
Phil 3:8-14.		
Jn 8:1-11.		

Readings	Theme	Approaches
Palm/Passion Sunday		
Year A	The Passion. *We*	Bringing the
Is 50:4-7.	*suggest the shortened*	message home:
Phil 2:6-11.	*version from The*	Start Easter story
Mt 26:14-27:66	*Children's Bible,*	book.
	or some part of it.	Easter Garden.
Year B	The Passion	Mime or drame
Is 50:4-7.		with props and
Phil 2:6-11.		costumes.
Mk 14:1-15; 47		
Year C	The Passion	Frieze.
Is 50:4-7		Tableau.
Phil 2:6-11		Liturgy board.
Lk 22:14-23; 56		

Season of Easter

Readings	Theme	Approaches
Easter Sunday	Mary of Magdala	Easter Garden.
Acts 10:34, 37-43.	discovers Jesus is gone	Sculpture tableau.
Col 3:1-4.	from the Tomb.	
Jn 20:1-9.		

Readings	Theme	Approaches
2nd Sunday of Easter		
Year A	Jesus appears to disciples in upper room. Doubting Thomas.	Easter Garden. Sculpture tableau.
Acts 2:42-47.		
1 Pet 1:3-9.		
Jn 20:19-31.		
Year B	Jesus in upper room.	Drama or mime with props and costumes.
Acts 4:32-35.		
1 Jn 5:1-6.		
Jn 20:19-31.		
Year C		Liturgy board.
Acts 5:12-16.		
Apoc 1:9-13, 17-19.		
Jn 20:19-31.		
3rd Sunday of Easter		
Year A	The road to Emmaus.	Story telling or mime.
Acts 2:14, 22-28.		
1 Pet 1:17-21.		
Lk 24:13-35.		
Year B	They recognise Jesus at the breaking of bread.	Story telling or mime with props and costumes.
Acts 3:13-15, 17-19.		
1 Jn 2:1-5.		
Lk 24:35-48.		
Year C	Jesus appears to the disciples fishing in the sea of Tiberius.	Liturgy board.
Acts 5:27-32, 40-41.		
Apoc 5:11-14.		
Jn 21:1-19.		
4th Sunday of Easter	I am the gate to the sheepfold.	Abstract: Story telling. Banners.
Year A		
Acts 2:14, 36-41.		
1 Pet 2:20-25.		
Jn 10:1-10.		
Year B	I know my own and my own know me.	Collage.
Acts 4:8-12.		
1 Jn 3:1-2.		
Jn 10:11-18.		

Readings	Theme	Approaches
Year C 　　Acts 13:14, 43-52. 　　Apoc 7:9, 14-17. 　　Jn 10:27-30.	I give eternal life to the sheep that belong to me.	Story telling. Collage banners.

5th Sunday of Easter

Readings	Theme	Approaches
Year A 　　Acts 6:1-7. 　　1 Pet 2:4-9. 　　Jn 14:1-12.	I am the Way, the Truth and the Life.	Liturgy board. Abstract themes.
Year B 　　Acts 9:26-31. 　　1 John 3:18-24. 　　Jn 15:1-8.	I am the vine, you are the branches.	Banners/collage.
Year C 　　Acts 14:21-27. 　　Apoc 21: 1-5. 　　Jn 13:31-35.	Love one another.	Story telling.

6th Sunday of Easter

Readings	Theme	Approaches
Year A 　　Acts 8:5-8, 14-17. 　　1 Peter 3:15-18. 　　Jn 14:15-21.	A promise of the coming of the spirit of truth. Keep my commandments.	Banners/collage.
Year B 　　Acts 10:25-26. 　　　　34-35, 44-48. 　　1 Jn 4:7-10. 　　Jn 15:9-17.	As the Father has loved me, so I love you.	Story telling.
Year C 　　Acts 15:1-2, 22-29. 　　Apoc 21:10-14, 22-23. 　　Jn 14:23-29.	The Holy Spirit will teach you everything.	Abstract themes. Bringing the message home.

Readings	Theme	Approaches
7th Sunday of Easter		

Year A
    Acts 1:12-14.
    1 Pet 4:13-16.
    Jn 17:1-11.
	Father, glorify your Son.	Abstract themes.

Year B
    Acts 1:15-17, 20-26.
    1 John 4:11-16.
    Jn 17:11-19.
	I passed your word on to them and the world hated them. /They are not of this world.	Story telling.

Year C
    Acts 7:55-60.
    Apoc 22:12-14,
        16-17, 20.
    Jn 17:20-26.
	May they all be one.	Bringing the message home.

Pentecost Sunday Acts 2:1-11. 1 Cor 12:3-7, 12-13. Jn 20:19-23.	The coming of the Holy Spirit.	Banners/collage. Frieze. Drawings to take home. Liturgy board.
Trinity Sunday		

Year A
    Ex 34:4-6, 8-9.
    2 Cor 13:11-13.
    Jn 3:16-18.
	God sent his Son that through him the world might be saved.	Story telling.

Year B
    Deut 4:32-34, 39-40.
    Rom 8:14-17.
    Mt 28:16-20.
	Jesus sent them out to baptise all nations.	Mime or drama.
		Liturgy board.

Year C
    Prov 8:22-31.
    Rom 5:1-5.
    Jn 16:12-15.
	The Spirit will lead you to the complete truth.	Story telling or dialogue.

Readings	Theme	Approaches

10th Sunday
of Ordinary Time
Year A
    Hosea 6:3-6.
    Rom 4:18-25.
    Mt 9:9-13.
	Jesus eats with the tax collectors and sinners.	Mime or drama.

Year B
    Gen 3:9-15.
    2 Cor 4:13, 5:1.
    Mk 3:20-35.
	The question of Satan.	Drawings.

Year C
    1 Kgs 17:17-24.
    Gal 1:11-19.
    Lk 7:11-17.
	Jesus restores a young man to life.	Story telling with props and costumes.

11th Sunday
Year A
    Ex 19:2-6.
    Rom 5:6-11.
    Mt 9:36, 10:8.
	Jesus sends the seventy-two disciples out to the harvest.	Mime or drama with props and costumes.

Year B
    Ezek 17:22-24.
    2 Cor 5:6-10.
    Mk 4:26-34.
	The parable of the mustard seed.	Puppets.

Year C
    2 Sam 12:7-10, 13.
    Gal 2:16, 19-21.
    Lk 7:36, 8:3.
	Mary Magdalen anoints Jesus' feet at Simon's house.	Collage of drawings.

12th Sunday
Year A
    Jer 20:10-13.
    Rom 5:12-15.
    Mt 10:26-33.
	Every hair on your head has been counted.	Story telling or dialogue.

Readings	Theme	Approaches
Year B Job 38:1, 8-11. 2 Cor 5:14-17. Mk 4:35-41.	Who can this be? Even the wind and the sea obey him.	Story telling or dialogue.
Year C Zech 12:10-11. Gal 3:26-29. Lk 9:18-24.	Who do you say I am?	Liturgy board.

13th Sunday

Year A 2 Kgs 4:8-11, 14-16. Rom 6:3-4, 8-11. Mt 10:37-42.	Anyone who welcomes you welcomes me.	Story telling. Liturgy board.
Year B Wis 1:13-15, 2:23-24. 2 Cor 8:7, 9, 13-15. Mk 5:21-43.	The cure of Jairus' daughter and the woman with the haemorrhage.	Mime or drama with props and costumes.
Year C 1 Kgs 19:16, 19-21. Gal 5:1, 13-18. Lk 9:51-62.	The Son of Man has nowhere to lay his head.	Mime or drama with props and costumes.

14th Sunday

Year A Zech 9:9-10. Rom 8:9, 11-13. Mt 11:25-30.	Come to me all you who labour and are over burdened.	Story telling.
Year B Ezek 2:2-5. 2 Cor 12:7-10. Mk 6:1-6.	A prophet is only despised in his own country.	Liturgy board.
Year C Is 66:10-14. Gal 6:14-18. Lk 10:1-22, 17-20.	The Lord sent them out in pairs.	Drama or mime.

Readings	Theme	Approaches
15th Sunday		
Year A	A sower went out	Drama or mime
Is 55:10-11.	to sow seed.	with props and
Rom 8:18-23.		costumes.
Mt 13:1-23.		
Year B	Jesus summoned the	Drama or mime
Amos 7:12-15.	twelve and sent them	with props and
Eph 1:3-14.	out in pairs.	costumes.
Mk 6:7-13.		
Year C	Who is my neigh-	Collage.
Deut 30:10-14.	bour?	Banners.
Col 1:15-20.		Abstract themes.
Lk 10:25-37.		
16th Sunday		
Year A	The darnel in the	Mime or drama.
Wis 12:13, 16-19.	field of wheat.	Drawings.
Rom 8:26-27.		
Mt 13:24-43.		
Year B	They were like sheep	Story telling with
Jer 23:1-6.	without a shepherd.	props.
Eph 2:13-18.		
Mk 6:30-34.		
Year C	Jesus visits Martha	Mime or drama.
Gen 18:1-10.	and Mary.	Liturgy board.
Col 1:24-28.		
Lk 10:38-42.		
17th Sunday		
Year A	The pearl of great	Story telling.
1 Kgs 3:5, 7-12.	price.	
Rom 8:28-30.	The kingdom of heav-	
Mt 13:44-52.	en is like ...	
Year B	The parable of the	Mime or drama.
2 Kgs 4:42-44.	loaves and fishes.	Liturgy board.
Eph 4:1-6.		
Jn 6:1-15.		

Readings	Theme	Approaches
Year C Gen 18:20-32. Col 2:12-24. Lk 11:1-13.	Lord teach us to pray. Knock and the door will be open to you.	Mime or drama. Liturgy board.
18th Sunday Year A Is 55:1-3. Rom 8:35, 37-39. Mt 14:13-21.	Parable of the loaves and fishes.	Mime with narrator. Banners.
Year B Ex 16:2-4, 12-15. Eph 4:17, 20-24. Jn 6:24-35.	I am the bread of life.	Story telling. Liturgy board.
Year C Ecc 1:2, 2:21-23. Col 3:1-5, 9-11. Lk 12:13-21.	Parable of the rich man who built barns to store his grain.	Mime with props and costumes. Puppets.
19th Sunday Year A 1 Kgs 19:9, 11-13. Rom 9:1-5. Mt 14:22-23.	Jesus walks on the water.	Mime or drama with props and costumes.
Year B 1 Kgs 19:4-8. Eph 4:30, 5:2. Jn 6:41-51.	I am the bread of life.	Banner. Collage
Year C Wis 18:6-9. Heb 11:1-2, 8-19. Lk 12:32-48.	Happy those servants whom the master finds awake when he comes.	Story telling. Puppets.

Readings	Theme	Approaches
20th Sunday		
Year A	Woman you have	Story telling.
Is 56:1, 6-7.	great faith.	Mime with
Rom 11:13-15,		narrator.
29-32.		
Mt 15:21-28.		
Year B	Jesus claims he	Abstract themes.
Prov 9:1-6.	is the bread of life.	Liturgy board.
Eph 5:15-20.		
Jn 6:51-58.		
Year C	I am not here to	Abstract themes.
Jer 38:4-6, 8-10.	bring peace, but	Banners.
Heb 12:1-4.	rather division.	
Lk 12:49-53.		
21st Sunday		
Year A	You are Peter and	Drama or mime
Is 22:19-23.	upon this rock I will	with costumes.
Rom 11:33-36.	build my church.	Liturgy board.
Mt 16:13-20.	Who do people say	
	the son of man is?	
Year B		
Josh 24:1-2, 15-18.	But there are some of	Abstract themes.
Eph 5:21-32.	you who do not	Story telling.
Jn 6:60-69.	believe.	
Year C	Try your best to enter	Abstract themes.
Is 66:18-21.	by the narrow door.	
Heb 12:5-7, 11-13.		
Lk 13:22-30.		
22nd Sunday		
Year A	Jesus prepares the	Story telling.
Jer 20:7-9.	disciples for what is to	Collage.
Rom 12:1-2.	come. /What then will	
Mt 16:21-27.	a man gain if he wins	
	the whole world	
	and loses his life.	

Readings	Theme	Approaches
Year B Deut 4:1-2, 6-8. Jas 1:17-18, 21-22, 27. Mk 7:1-8, 14-15, 21-23.	Jesus teaches about law and tradition. It is the things that come out of a man that make him unclean.	Story telling. Collage.
Year C Ecc 3:17-20, 28-29. Heb 12:18-19, 22-24. Lk 14:1, 7-14.	He who exalts himself will be humbled.	Mime. Puppets.

23rd Sunday

Year A Ezek 33:7-9. Rom 13:8-10. Mt 18:15-20.	Where two or three meet in my name I shall be there with them.	Story telling. Mime.
Year B Is 35:4-7. Jas 2:1-5. Mk 7:31-37.	Jesus cures the deaf man.	Mime or drama with props and costumes.
Year C Wis 9:13-18. Phlm 9-10, 12-17. Lk 14:25-33.	Give up all your possessions to follow Jesus.	Puppets.

24th Sunday

Year A Ecc 27:30, 28:7. Rom 14:7-9. Mt 18:21-35.	Forgive seventy-times seven.	Mime or drama with props and costumes.
Year B Is 50:5-9. Jas 2:14-18. Mk 8:27-35.	Who do people say I am?	Mime. Drawing. Collage.

Readings	Theme	Approaches

Year C
    Ex 32:7-11, 13-14.
    1 Tim 1:12-17.
    Lk 15:1-32.
	They will rejoice in
	heaven over one
	repentant sinner.
		Story telling.
		Mime.
		Liturgy board.

Readings	Theme	Approaches

25th Sunday
Year A
    Is 55:6-9.
    Phil 1:20-24, 27.
    Mt 20:1-16.
	Hiring workers
	for the vineyard.
		Mime with
		narrator, props
		and costumes.

Year B
    Wis 2:12, 17-20.
    Jas 3:16, 4:3.
    Mk 9:30-37.
	The first shall be last.
	Welcome little children.
		Mime or drama.
		Liturgy board.

Year C
    Amos 8:4-7.
    1 Tim 2:1-8.
    Lk 16:1-13.
	You cannot be the slave
	of both God and money.
		Collage.
		Puppets.

Readings	Theme	Approaches

26th Sunday
Year A
    Ez 18:25-28.
    Phil 2:1-11.
    Mt 21:28-32.
	Which of the two sons
	did the fathers will?
		Puppets.
		Story telling.

Year B
    Num 11:25-29.
    Jas 5:1-6.
    Mk 9:38-43,
        45, 47-48.
	If your hand should
	cause you to sin cut it
	off.
		Story telling.
		Dialogue.

Year C
    Amos 6:1, 4-7.
    1 Tim 6:11-16.
    Lk 16:19-31.
	Lazarus at the rich man's
	gate.
		Mime.
		Puppets.

Readings	Theme	Approaches
27th Sunday		
Year A Is 5:1-7. Phil 4:6-9. Mt 21:33-43.	The tenants rebel against the owner and take over the vineyard.	Drama or mime. Puppets.
Year B Gen 2:18-24. Heb 2:9-11. Mk 10:2-16.	Marriage and divorce.	Abstract themes.
Year C Hab 1:2-3, 2:2-4. 2 Tim 1:6-8, 13-14. Lk 17:5-10.	If you had faith the size of a mustard seed!	Props. Drawings. Collage. Story telling.
28th Sunday		
Year A Is 25:6-10. Phil 4:12-14, 19-20. Mt 22:1-14.	Many are called but few are chosen. The wedding feast.	Mime with narrator, props and costumes.
Year B Wis 7:7-11. Heb 4:12-13. Mk 10:17-30.	What must I do to inherit eternal life?	Mime with narrator.
Year C 2 Kgs 5:14-17. 2 Tim 2:8-13. Lk 17:11-19.	Jesus cures the ten lepers.	Mime with narrator, props and costumes.
29th Sunday		
Year A Is 45:1, 4-6. 1 Thess 1:1-5. Mt 22:15-21.	Give to Caesar what belongs to Caesar and to God what belongs to God.	Story telling and dialogue.

Readings	Theme	Approaches
Year B Is 53:10-11. Heb 4:14-16. Mk 10:35-45.	Anyone who wants to become great among you must be your servant.	Story telling and dialogue.
Year C Ex 17:8-13. 2 Tim 3:14, 4:2. Lk 18:1-8.	The widow pesters the judge for justice.	Mime with narrator.

30th Sunday

Year A Ex 22:20-26. 1 Thes 1:5-10. Mt 22:34-50.	The first two commandments.	Collage. Liturgy board on love.
Year B Jer 31:7-9. Heb 5:1-6. Mk 10:46-52.	Jesus cures Bartimaeus the blind beggar.	Mime or drama with props and costumes.
Year C Ecc 35:12-14, 16-19. 2 Tim 4:6-8, 16-18. Lk 18:9-14.	The Pharisee and the tax collector pray in the Temple.	Puppets or mime.

31st Sunday

Year A Mal 1:14, 2:2, 8-10. 1 Thes 2:7-9, 13. Mt 23:1-12.	They do not practice what they preach.	Story telling. Abstract themes.
Year B Deut 6:2-6. Heb 7:23-28. Mk 12:28-34.	The first two commandments.	Liturgy board. Drawings to take home.
Year C Wis 11:22, 12:2. 2 Thes 1:11, 2:2. Lk 19:1-10.	Zacchaeus.	Mime or drama. Puppets.

Readings	Theme	Approaches
32nd Sunday		
Year A	Ten bridesmaids took	Drama or mime
Wis 6:12-16.	their lamps and went	with props.
1 Thes 4:13-18.	to meet the bride-	Collage on
Mt 25:1-13.	groom.	generosity.
Year B	The widow's mite.	Mime with
1 Kgs 17:10-16.		narrator.
Heb 9:24-28.		Puppets.
Mk 12:38-44.		
Year C	The question of the	Story telling.
2 Macc 7:1-2, 9-14.	widow and the seven	Abstract themes.
2 Thes 2:16, 3:5.	brothers-in-law.	
Lk 20:27-38.		
33rd Sunday		
Year A	The parable	Collage.
Prov 31:10-13,	of the talents.	Mime with props,
19-20, 30-31.		costumes and
1 Thes 5:1-6.		narrator.
Mt 25:14-30.		Puppets.
Year B	Heaven and earth will	Story telling.
Daniel 12:1-3.	pass away but my	Abstract themes.
Heb 10:11-14, 18.	words will not pass	
Mk 13:24-32.	away.	
Year C	Your endurance will	Liturgy board.
Mal 3:19-20.	win you your lives.	
2 Thes 3:7-12.		
Lk 21:5-19.		
34th Sunday:		
The Lord Jesus Christ,		
Universal King		
Year A	I was hungry	Collage.
Ezek 34:11-12, 15-17.	and you gave me food.	Mime or drama
1 Cor 15:20-26, 28.		with narrator.
Mt 25:31-46.		

Readings	Theme	Approaches
Year B	It is you who say	
Dan 7: 13-14.	that I am king.	Abstract themes.
Apoc 1:5-8.		Liturgy board.
Jn 18:33-37.		
Year C	Lord, remember me	Tableau.
2 Sam 5:1-3.	when you come into	Mime with props
Col 1:11-20.	your kingdom.	and narrator.
Lk 23:35-43.		